SUMMARY

OF

THE ART OF WAR.

SUMMARY

OF

THE ART OF WAR:

WRITTEN

EXPRESSLY FOR AND DEDICATED TO

THE U. S. VOLUNTEER ARMY.

BY

EMIL SCHALK, A. O.

PHILADELPHIA:
J. B. LIPPINCOTT & CO.
1862.

Entered, according to the Act of Congress, in the year 1862, by

J. B. LIPPINCOTT & CO.,

In the Clerk's Office of the District Court of the United States for the Eastern District of Pennsylvania.

CONTENTS.

	PAGE
I. Art of War	9
II. Strategy	12
Base of Operation	12
Lines of Communication	13
Lines of Operation	13
Offensive Operations	17
Defensive Operations	20
Example—War in the United States	25
III. Grand Tactics	55
ARMIES	58
Elements composing them	58
Infantry	58
Cavalry	61
Artillery	62
Organization	66
Normal Arrangement of Troops for Battle	72
BATTLES—FIGHTS—SKIRMISHES	80
Defensive Battles	81
Defensive Battles with Offensive Returns	82
Offensive Battles	84
Orders of Battle	91
Examples—Battle of the Alma	96
Battle of Wagram	101
Battle of Leuthen	102
Battle of Prague	104
Battle of Talavera	106
Battle of Austerlitz	107

CONTENTS.

	PAGE
USE OF THE THREE ARMS, COMBINED OR SEPARATE	109
Infantry	110
Cavalry	113
Artillery	116
Each of the Three Arms in the Attack or Defense	116
The Three Arms Combined in the Attack or Defense	121
Example—Battle of Waterloo	136

IV. Mixed Operations ... 150
    PASSAGE OF RIVERS ... 150
        Example—Passage of the Limmat by Massena ... 154
    RETREAT AND PURSUIT ... 163
    DESCENTS AND EXPEDITIONS ... 167

V. Logistics ... 173
    Example—March and Manœuvres near Jena, 1806 ... 179
        March and Manœuvres near Ulm, 1805 ... 180

PREFACE.

FEW nations, if any, in the world, would have been able to accomplish what the people of this great country have done. Within three or four months, an army larger than that possessed by any of the great powers of Europe has been raised, armed, equipped, drilled, and put in the field. Men of all classes, rich and poor, have entered the ranks; and there is scarcely any quiet occupation which has not furnished its share of officers and privates. The merchant and the lawyer, yesterday at their desks, to-day command regiments and armies. If we can only admire this great national movement and the patriotism which has caused it, we may perhaps be allowed to make a few observations the importance of which every intelligent officer will admit.

Bravery is a national virtue of the American, and we certainly do not doubt that of the officers of the great army; but bravery is not sufficient to gain victories. War is a science, and a difficult one. History is full of examples of the weak defeating the strong by superiority of knowledge in conducting troops. In drilling, we learn but the figures which troops may form; but we do not learn their application: therefore every officer should know the great principles of war, which will teach him how to approach the enemy, and, when in his presence, how to apply the figures of the drill.

I have undertaken, in this little work, to give a clear and precise idea of the great maxims of war. It was written for the citizen soldier and officer. To show the application of the principles, I have given several examples fully developed. My intention was not to write anything new, nor to give a learned dissertation on military matters, but simply to fill up the void that exists, by a popular work treating those military matters, of easy understanding even to the civilian who has never before been connected with military occupations. The professed officer who takes this book in hand must, therefore, excuse, if it does not realize his ideas of a precise treatise on the art of war. Those who wish to instruct themselves more fully in the art of conducting troops must consult other and more special works.

THE ART OF WAR.

EVERY war is undertaken to obtain a certain object.

A war is a calamity; therefore the means giving the speediest attainment of our object are the best.

Only preconcerted and precise plans, in accordance with the rules of the military sciences, with our means and those of the enemy, with the configuration of the theater of war, will permit an energetic action, and, in consequence, a speedy termination of the war.

War can be offensive, purely defensive, or defensive with offensive return.

Offensive wars, if properly conducted, have many advantages; purely defensive ones will always end with submission.

Defensive, with offensive return, may be accompanied with great results.

The rules which ought to guide us in the adoption of our plans are defined in the military sciences called:—

1st. **Strategy,** or the art of directing the masses of our army on the theater of war for the attainment of our object.

2d. **Grand Tactics,** or the art to move and dispose of troops in the presence of the enemy.

3d. **Logistics**, or the art of arranging our movements.

4th. The **Art of Engineering**, defense and attack of places.

5th. **Tactics of each Arm.**

Every war is composed of marches, battles, sieges, erection of fortifications, and pauses of repose.

Each of these separate operations is to be conducted in accordance with the strict rules laid down in one of the five separate sciences.

The entire war, composed of these different operations, may be looked at as a great drama, in which these different operations form the different acts.

As soon as our armies are ready to take the field, the nature of the war is to be fixed—if offensive, if defensive, or if of the offensive defense.

The next care will be the study of the theater of the war.

It will then be upon the rules of strategy upon which we must fix our base of operation, our lines of advance or retreat, our manœuvres, our different objects before the attainment of the final and main object, our lines of defense, our places of refuge in case of defeat.

Our manœuvers and marches will conduct us, sooner or later, in the presence of the enemy; it is then, by the rules of grand tactics, that we learn how to displace or destroy the obstacles the enemy puts in our way in the shape of his army.

In the application of grand tactics, we use certain figures and forms by which we dispose of our different army corps to enable them better to sustain the shock of the two masses.

Those figures and forms are given in the small tactics of every country.

Our strategical movements may conduct us to overcome natural and artificial difficulties which we find in our way, as, for instance, rivers, fortifications, etc. It is then that the art of engineering will find its employment; and, finally, to arrive from one point to another, we must march in a certain order, we must be provided with provision and ammunition, and their logistics will tell us how to make our different arrangements.

There are three great maxims common to the whole science of war; they are—

1st. Concentrate your force, and act with the whole of it on one part only of the enemy's force.

2d. Act against the weakest part of your enemy—his center, if he is dispersed; his flank or rear, if concentrated. Act against his communications without endangering your own.

3d. Whatever you do, as soon as you have made your plan, and taken the decision to act upon it, act with the utmost speed, so that you may obtain your object before the enemy suspects what you are about.

STRATEGY.

It is impossible to give here a full account of all the expressions and rules of strategy. I shall only mention the principal ones, and then at once proceed, by an example, to show how strategical combinations may be conducted.

Base of Operation.—Upon entering into a war, we must have a line for the concentration of our troops, where we

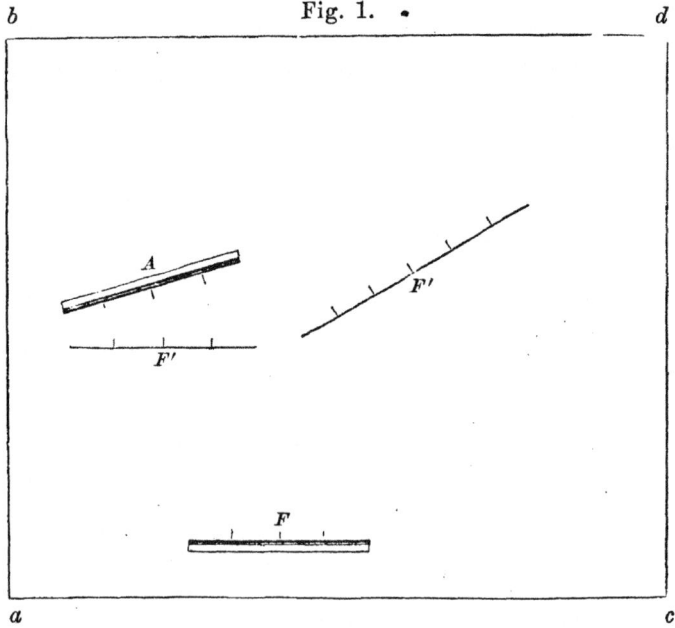

Fig. 1.

have our depots and magazines, and from which we advance to execute our different plans. This line is called *base of operation.* The first choice of this line is of the utmost importance. The result of a whole campaign may depend on it. If, for instance, *a b c d* is the theater of the war, if *a c* and *a b* belong to us, if *b d* is the sea, the army of the enemy has for sole retreat *c d*. We may choose *a b* or *a c* for our base. In choosing *a b*, the enemy's army would always have its retreat to *c d* free. But, in choosing *a c*, we may advance from F to F', cut the army A from its communications, force it in the corner, *b*, where it would be obliged to surrender; that is, if our tactical arrangements are, in the engagements, as superior as the strategical were in the directions, one battle and the fate of a state is decided. The battle of Jena, in 1806, is an example of this.

Or, if *a b* is our base, *c d* that of the enemy, we might advance from *m* to *c* without fear of being driven from our communications, while the enemy would even be endangered by advancing on the straight line *m n*; because we would always be able to retreat to *a*, but the enemy, having only a small base, will expose his own communications as soon as he tries to act on ours. See Fig. 2.

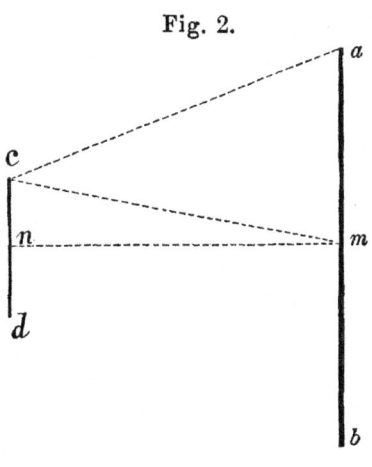

Fig. 2.

Lines of Communication are called the lines joining us to our base or to another army, which co-operates with us on the same theater of war.

Lines of Operation.—If the base of operation is of importance, the lines of operation are still more so. We call the *line of operation* of an army the line which the principal body of the army follows. If there is but one army on the same frontier, the line would be simple; if there are two armies, there would be a double line of operation.

The interior line of operation is the line which two or more armies would follow, if attacked from different sides by different armies, but so that they would be enabled to join before the corps of the enemy could do so. The way from a to b, in Fig. 3, would be the interior line; the way from c to d, the exterior line.

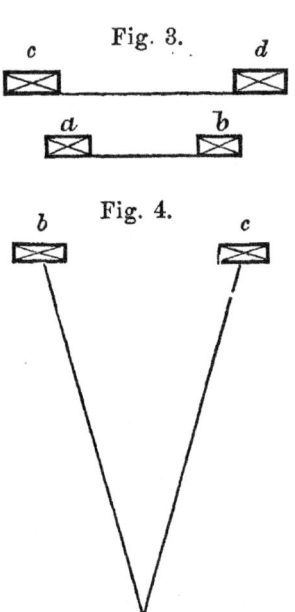

We call, likewise, *concentric lines* the lines of two or more armies or army corps, parting from distant points and meeting together in one point. See Fig. 4. Divergent lines leave one point to arrive at two or three distant points. If leaving a, $a\,b$ and $a\,c$ are divergent lines; if b and c, they are concentric ones.

If an army is placed between two hostile armies, so that it can defeat each of them before they are able to make a junction, its position is called a central one.

Besides the definitions already given, we call strategic points and lines all such points and lines situated on the theater of war the occupation of which may be of importance during the war.

STRATEGY.

We call *lines of defense* all such lines which we choose for our defense, or which by the natural configuration permit of an easy defense. It is evident that the line must be a strategic one—that is, it must be so situated that by its occupation we prevent the enemy attaining his object. No one would call the crest of a mountain entirely out of the way a line of defense, though it might be easily defended.

Each theater of war can be divided into the three zones —right, left, and center.

As general maxims of strategy we might name the following:—

1st. To turn to the best advantage the reciprocal direction of our base of operation and that of the enemy.

2d. To choose the one of the three zones of the theater of war on which we can bring the greatest disasters to the enemy with the least risk to ourselves.

Example: Fig. 5. If $a\ b\ c\ d$ is the theater of the war, if the enemy has three armies, m, m', m'', disposed in the three different zones, and if, for instance, our means of concentration were such that we could concentrate in one of those zones nearly the whole of our force before the enemy could reinforce this zone, we would be obliged to choose it, as it would at once give us a decided superiority in the following operations. If no other consideration were to prevail, the center would be the most advantageous point to act on, as it would at once divide the force of the enemy, and render a junction of m and m'' impossible.

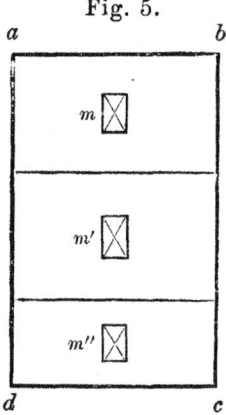

Fig. 5.

3d. To well direct the lines of operation in defense as well as attack, the interior lines are always to be adopted. In the defense, those lines ought to be concentric; in the attack, which is just the opposite, they ought to be divergent.

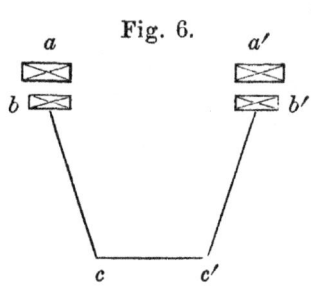

Fig. 6.

Example for defense, Fig. 6 : a and a' attack b and b'; a is stronger than b, and a' is stronger than b'; but $b+b'$ are stronger than a or a'; therefore b and b' retreat by $b\,c$ and $b'\,c'$ to c and c', followed by a and a'; arrived at c and c', they make a junction by the line $c\,c'$, and fall on a and then on a', defeating each separately by their superior force. $b\,c$ and $b'\,c'$ are the concentric lines, $c\,c'$ is the interior line.

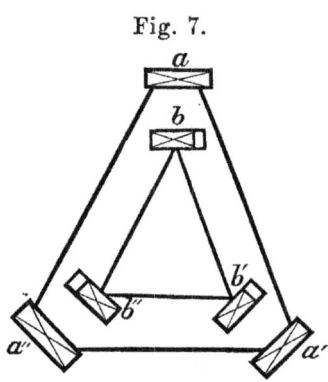

Fig. 7.

Or, if a, a', a'' are attacking b, b', b'', Fig. 7, the latter can always unite by the interior lines, $b\,b'$, $b'b''$, and $b\,b''$, before a, a', a'' can do so by their exterior lines; b, b', and b'' may, therefore, though each one being weaker than the army opposed to it, defeat a, a', a'', by uniting successively their masses on the three different points, and by attacking with their superior force each of the enemy's armies separately.

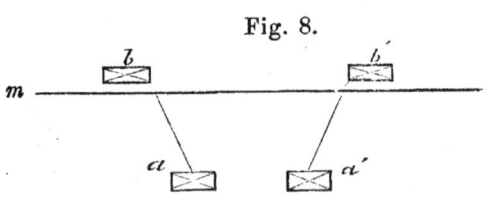

Fig. 8.

Example for the attack, Fig. 8: Let $m\,n$ be the frontier of a country, b and b' the position of the defending armies; the attacking parties ought to choose the position a and a', and advance on the lines $a\,b$ and $a'\,b'$, so as to separate b from b', and to obtain an interior position between them; $a\,b$ and $a'\,b'$ are then divergent lines.

4th. No. 3 implies that we ought to choose our lines so that we can always unite our divisions before the enemy can unite his, and that with our united force we ought to defeat him in detail. The examples of No. 3 will suffice to explain this.

5th. To give the troops the utmost activity and speed.

The above-mentioned rules are the most important of strategy; there only remains to be shown the general dispositions for defensive or offensive campaigns.

Offensive Operations.

Whatever be the form of the theater of war, it can be divided into three zones—right, left, and center; a choice is to be made in which of the three zones the operations are to take place.

Circumstances may be such that one, two, or even the three zones may be employed; in the first case we would have a simple line, in the two others several lines, of operation.

1st. If there is but one line, two cases may occur—either that the enemy is dispersed or occupies a very extended line, or that he holds a concentrated position.

In the first case, the most advantageous point to act on is the center, which we should break with our whole force, and then defeat each of the two wings separately.

In 1796, Napoleon, when opposed to Beaulieu, whose

line was extended from Genoa to Ceva, broke through the center of the Austrian army at Montenotte with his entire army, and then defeated, one after the other, the two wings, in the engagements of Milesimo Dego and Mondovi.

In 1809, when opposed to the Archduke Charles, whose army also formed a very extended line, he acted in a similar way, and defeated, successively, the Austrian forces in the battles of Abensberg, Eckmuhl, Landshut, and Ratisbon.

In the second case, if the enemy keeps his forces concentrated, the manœuvre against his center is rendered impossible, or at least not advantageous, and we should see if the attack on one of the three zones does not present the chance of our acting at once on the enemy's communications without endangering our own. The figures 1 and 2 will show how this is possible. When once on the enemy's communications, we close his line of retreat; to return to his base, he is obliged to force his way with the bayonet; if he fails in this attempt and is defeated, he will be forced to surrender. Examples of such operations are the campaigns of 1800, 1805, and 1806.

In 1805, Mack, with an Austrian army, near Ulm, was turned by Napoleon, and obliged to capitulate. This result was obtained in consequence of the position and extension of the two bases of operation. Fig. 2 will explain this, by supposing that $a\,b$ forms the base of the French, (the Rhine,) and that they advance from a to n, and cut the Austrian army, which has advanced in the direction of m, from its base, $c\,d$.

In 1806, the Prussians were also cut from their communications, obliged to fight at Jena and Auerstadt, front against Prussia; they were defeated, and the remainder of their army obliged to lay down arms, as they found their line of retreat continually closed by Napoleon's division advancing parallel with them in the direction of the Baltic Sea. In Fig. 1 we have but to replace $a\ c$ by the River Maine, $a\ b$ by the Rhine, and $c\ d$ by the Baltic Sea. A would be the Prussian army, which has for sole retreat $c\ d$. F is the first, and F' the second, position of the French.

Should the enemy, however, keep such a position that neither the manœuvres against his center nor against his communications are possible, then it is necessary to resort to stratagems which shall induce him to make wrong movements, divide his troops, extend his line, etc.

For instance, we may give our whole army such a position, or we may, before the commencement of the operations, place our army corps in such a manner, that they can act with the same facility against very distant points.

The enemy is obliged to make a division of his force, and our first position must be chosen in a way that, in fact, we may by a few forced and hidden marches, unite our entire army on the decisive point, and defeat the enemy in detail.

2d. If we form two lines of operation, we should follow divergent lines—that is, we should place our armies between those of the enemy, and transport our main body alternately from one army to the other. The enemy's armies, being isolated, cannot unite, and must fall under the blows of our superior force.

The plan of the campaign of 1800, as devised by Napoleon, is the finest example that can be offered for a similar operation.

Melas, with a large army in Italy, had arrived at a short distance from the French frontier; Kray, with another army, threatened the Rhine. Moreau, near Basel, was to act against Kray; and the reserve army, disposed on the Swiss frontier, was to act in Italy. Napoleon's plan was for Moreau to pass through Switzerland, cross the Rhine at Schaffhausen, to cut Kray from his communications, and thereby destroy his army, while Napoleon crossed the Alps by the passages of the Great St. Bernard, Simplon, St. Gothard, and Spluegen, and arrived in the rear of Melas.

Moreau did not entirely conform to Napoleon's plan; he crossed the Rhine near Basel, where he was already in possession of a tete-de-pont, and therefore the campaign in Germany was not so decisive as that in Italy. Melas found himself turned, and was obliged to fight at Marengo, front against Austria; he was defeated, and consequently compelled to enter into a convention with Napoleon, by which the latter obtained the western portion of Italy as far as the Mincio.

The battle of Marengo, and even the whole of Napoleon's manœuvre, took place only after he had received a reinforcement of 15,000 men from Moreau.

Defensive Operations.

We may be offensive in the operations, even though the war is defensive for us. This will always be the case, if we are sooner ready to take the field than the enemy; if his dispositions are faulty, his army corps dispersed, etc., or if in general our numerical superiority is very great. The initiative is always advantageous, and we decide upon taking the defensive only in case of an inferiority in strength.

The defense can act, as well as the offensive, on simple or several lines of operation; it is always more intimately connected with the configuration of the ground than the attack. In the defense, the natural or artificial obstacles of the country should supply the deficiency of men, either in strategical or tactical operations. When acting on simple lines, and opposed only to one, but a superior, army of the enemy, our own army should retreat in defending all the natural obstacles of the theater of the war, such as rivers, mountains, etc.; it should organize small bodies for acting in the rear of the advancing enemy, to endanger his convoys and force him to make large detachments to cover them.

In making those detachments, the invading army becomes smaller the more it advances, while, on the other hand, the defending army generally gets stronger the nearer it approaches the center of its country. If by this the difference in force is decreased, and the chances more equal, the army for the defense should pass to a vigorous offensive, either by unexpectedly attacking the enemy or by awaiting him in a well-chosen, strong, and fortified position. The campaign of 1812 is a fine example of such a defense.

Napoleon entered Russia with 450,000 men. The Russian army retreated, defending only the town of Smolensk; by the many detachments Napoleon was obliged to make, and the losses already sustained, he arrived at Borodino with only 132,000 men. The Russians awaited him there, in a partly fortified position, with 117,000 men. What was impossible to do against an army of 450,000 men could be tried against one of 132,000.

When the enemy has chosen two lines of operation, we may be induced to take but one line, and bring our army in a central position between his armies, so as to fall with our whole force on the first of his corps that presents itself, and then defeat the others.

At the siege of Mantua, in 1796, Napoleon, being informed that Wurmser, who had advanced from the Tyrol against him, had divided his force and was descending one bank of the Lake of Garda with his main body, while Quasdanowich was descending the other, raised the siege of Mantua, advanced, and stationed himself at one end of the lake, thereby gaining a central position, and separating Wurmser from Quasdanowich; the latter is first defeated, at Lonato, and the former at Castiglione.

If obliged to form several lines of operation, we arrange them in the following manner:—

If, for instance, 100,000 men are to resist an invading army of 150,000 men, divided in three armies of 50,000 each, we should divide our force also. We form three corps of observation, each numbering 15,000 men. We keep the remaining 55,000 in reserve, and transport them successively by interior lines and forced marches to the three army corps, and form every time a large army of 70,000 men, who should defeat the 50,000 opposed to them.

The two remaining corps of observation, if pressed by

their opponents, retreat, defending every inch of ground, but refusing open battle, till they are in turn reinforced by the reserve army. In those cases, the defense loses ground, but soon regains it.

If the enemy has formed double lines of operation, very distant from each other, we should also form two lines, and retreat on concentric ones, as shown in Fig. 6 ; when we arrive at c and c', only a few days' march from each other, we leave a corps of observation before one of the enemy's armies, in order to mask our movements, and, with our main body, we reach by forced marches our other army, unite with it, and defeat the enemy by our superiority ; we then return to the first army, the fate of which will not remain long undecided.

In 1796, the Archduke Charles, in Germany, defeated the armies of Jordan and Moreau by retreating on concentric lines from the Rhine to the Bohemian frontier. To Jordan was opposed Wartensleben, with about 30,000 men. The Archduke Charles commanded in person the army opposed to Moreau ; arrived near the Lech, he left General Latour, with 30,000 men, and, with the remainder of his army, he joined Wartensleben, after some forced marches at Amberg, where he defeated Jordan ; he pursued and defeated him a second time at Würzburg, and a third time on the Lahn ; he then left a corps to continue the pursuit, while he himself turned against Moreau, and marched to cut him from his line of retreat. The news that the archduke had left the army opposed to him reached Moreau only after Jordan's defeat ; he then commenced to retreat, but was overtaken by the duke, and defeated at Emmendingen and

Schlingen, and forced again to cross the Rhine—an operation which had already been executed by Jordan.

In the years 1758 to 1762, Frederick the Great was attacked by a Russian, Austrian, and German Imperial army. He resisted those three armies by disposing his own exactly as shown in Fig. 7 ; he always transported the mass of his force to the most endangered point by means of the interior lines which he held, and defeated the different armies one after the other, and came victorious out of a war unequaled in history.

In the years 1813 and 1814, Napoleon, in his defense also acted on interior lines.

This short exposé of strategy will be sufficient to give a general idea of this science, and to make the following example understood.

Those who wish to obtain an entire knowledge of strategy, and the operations attached to it, may consult *Jomini's Art of War*, recently translated from the French by Captain Mendell and Lieutenant Craighill, U. S. Army.

EXAMPLE.

WAR IN THE UNITED STATES.

IF I choose the rebellious States for the theater of war in my example, I do it only because I know that such an example will be more interesting to my readers than any of the most beautiful strategical operations in Europe. But I must say at once that, in giving this example, I will only give a general idea how the principles of strategy might be applied; but I am far from making any allusion to facts which have happened or might happen. Besides, I choose my example without consideration of the actual position of the two belligerent parties; and I must also say, that I make no pretension to give the different movements as they should perhaps be, if made in accordance with a thorough knowledge of the country. In short, I adopt imaginary armies, and I suppose them equally brave and equally well organized; and I trace the movements on a very incomplete map, after only a very superficial study of this map.

The northern boundaries of Virginia, Kentucky, and the north and east boundaries of Missouri, form, in my supposition, the boundaries of the two belligerent parties.

The object of the war is the extinction of rebellion.

Rebellion can only be extinguished by the destruction of its armies and the occupation of its territory.

Occupation can only be the result of offensive movements; therefore the nature of the war will be offensive for the North, and ought to be of an offensive defense for the South.

The attack requires greater force than the defense.

Therefore we suppose the armies of the North to be larger than those of the South. Let the one be 700,000, and the other 500,000 men.

The war is to be finished in the shortest time.

The 700,000 Union troops, divided into several armies, have to destroy or disperse the 500,000 soldiers of the South, and to advance into the very heart of the rebellious States.

The general plan of operation, as devised by the government of the North, we suppose to be as follows:—

1st. A. — Army of the Potomac, 200,000 men.
  Base of operation, the Potomac.
  Orders: to take Richmond, to advance to North Carolina, and to occupy Georgia.

2d. A^I. — Army of Fort Monroe, 100,000 men.
  Base of operation, Fort Monroe.
  Orders: to co-operate with A.

3d. A^{II}. — Reserve army, 75,000 men, divided in the depots, arsenals, forts, towns, sea-ports, etc. of the Eastern States.

4th. A^{III}. — Kentucky army, 100,000 men.
  Base of operation, the Ohio.
  Orders: to clear Kentucky and Tennessee of the rebels, and to advance to Alabama.

5th. A^{IV}. — Army of Missouri, 100,000 men.
Base of operation, the Mississippi.
Orders: to clear Missouri and Arkansas of the rebels, to advance to the South, to cross the Mississippi, and to occupy New Orleans.

6th. A^{V}. — Reserve army for the Kentucky and Missouri armies, 50,000 men, distributed on the passages across the Mississippi and Ohio.

7th. A^{VI}. — Army of Port Royal, 50,000 men.
Base of operation, United States fleet.
Orders: to occupy South Carolina.

8th. A^{VII}.—Army of Western Virginia, 25,000 men.
Base of operation, the Ohio.
Orders: to occupy Western Virginia.

The position of these different armies, as well as their projected lines of operations, are shown in the map.

Opposed to them are—

1st. To the Potomac army the rebel army, B, 175,000 men.

2d. To Fort Monroe army the rebel army B^{I}, 60,000 men.

3d. Reserve of B and B^{I} disposed near Richmond, B^{II}, 20,000 men.

4th. Opposed to the Kentucky army is B^{III}, numbering 80,000 men.

5th. Opposed to the Missouri army is B^{IV}, 80,000 men.

6th. Reserve of B^{III} and B^{IV} is B^{V}, distributed near the Memphis and Huntsville railway line, 50,000 men.

7th. Opposed to Port Royal army is B^{VI}, 15,000 men.

8th. Opposed to the Western Virginian army is B^{VII}, 20,000 men.

The position of these armies at the commencement of the operations is shown in the map.

The plan of the North seems grand; to each rebel army a larger union army is opposed, and the fate of the rebellion seems to be decided in a few months.

The commanders of the different armies have received their orders, and the operations commence.

Each commander has different objects to obtain; his main object is to carry out his order, his nearer one the destruction of the obstacles in his way.

Each commander, therefore, traces his own plans, but, being only part of *one* great plan, he ought to co-operate in his arrangements as much as possible with the armies nearest to him.

Let us begin with the operations of the Potomac and Fort Monroe armies. These two armies have to co-operate; and they have for main object the taking of Richmond and the occupation of Virginia, North Carolina, and Georgia. Their nearest object is the destruction of the armies B, B^I, and B^{II}.

A and A^I united are stronger than the three rebel armies B, B^I, and B^{II}, and therefore their action should be simultaneous, to engage at one and the same moment the whole and inferior rebel armies.

Considering the difference between A and A^I, we conclude that A^I plays a more subordinate rôle than A. It is, in fact, nothing else than a great detachment of this army.

The action of A^I has therefore more the character of a diversion in favor of A, than that of a separate and main operation.

If B is kept in continual expectation of being attacked by A, it cannot move; and if, at the same time, A^I attacks B^I, and defeats it by its superior force, B will either be obliged to give up its line of defense or to send a part of its force to the reinforcement of B^I, and then the moment for the main attack by A has arrived.

To act a diversion—that is, to make the enemy commit the fault of a division of his forces—the diversion must have the appearance of a main operation; it must be directed on the weak parts of the enemy, and, as it never acts with sufficient forces, the energy of its action and the speed and daring of its movements must supply the want of men.

Therefore the advance of A^I from Fort Monroe must be impetuous, irresistible; whatever may be its loss, whatever may be the difficulties on its way, A^I must surmount them. It must defeat the army opposed to it, force its way through any obstacle, and must arrive at Williamsburg, from whence it has to proceed to Kent and Richmond. This last town is to be taken by assault; and as soon as this is accomplished, A^I has fulfilled its nearest object—that is, the diversion; it should, therefore, fall back, and take up its position in advance of Williamsburg, so that it cannot be cut off from its base, but may still reach Richmond in one forced march, or recommence the action as soon as the circumstances require its doing so.

A has advanced at the same time that A^I has, and threatens B with an attack; B, in the expectation of a battle, cannot easily make a detachment, but, hearing of B^I's defeat, and the danger of B^{II} and of its own lines of communication, it will be obliged either to retreat entirely, and to leave its line of defense to A, or to support B^I and B^{II} by sending them a strong reinforcement. In the first case, the nearest object of A is obtained without battle; in the second, the moment B has divided, its force will be made use of by A to make with its concentrated force an attack on the weakened B. B's line of defense will be carried; A advances, pushing B before it, arrives near Richmond; the action of A^I recommences, it acts against the wing and rear of the already defeated and strongly pressed army B; complete rout of B would be the consequence, and the taking of Richmond and the attainment of the main object would be an easy matter.

This, or similar, would be the plan of attack; this plan, on the whole, is easily imagined by the rebel leaders, through the concentration of the Union forces, and their object is to prevent its execution.

The rebel armies B, B^I, and B^{II}, being inferior to A and A^I united, but superior to A or A^I, have to act with their whole force against each one separately. Therefore, if the whole plan of A and A^I—that is, of the attack—is based on a simultaneous action, action in one and the same moment of time, the plan of the defense must be based on a consecutive action, or action in two consecutive moments of time. To bring those two consecutive moments of time as near as possible to each other, the rebels, in their defense, have to make the best use of their central position, and they have to complete their interior lines of communication, as would be a railway from Manassas Junction to Fredericksburg, and one from Bowling Green to King William. To make their successive action possible, if even A and A^I act simultaneously, they have to oppose such artificial obstacles to the advance of A and A^I that they would be enabled to act with their main body against the one of the two which offers the first chance, while the other is occupied with the surmounting of those artificial obstacles. The amount of those obstacles must be calculated by the time the rebels need to pass from one action to the other. B's line of defense should be put in such a condition that, even with a very inferior force, it might be maintained for some time against A's very superior force—at all events, long enough to permit of B acting with a part of its force against A^I without exposing the remainder of its army to a total defeat or destruction; and so B^I would arrange several lines of defense, one behind the other, that it might hinder the advance of A^I, or at least prepare it such losses, and reduce its numerical superiority in such a serious manner, that the final destruction of it would be a matter of comparative ease, and could be accomplished with only a small detachment of B.

A and A^I begin their action; they leave their respective bases on one and the same day. A advances in the direction of Manassas Junction, and will arrive, at the end of about one day's march, near the rebel's position there. The distance from Manassas Junction to Richmond is about 100 miles, and can therefore be reached in five days' march. From Fort Monroe to Richmond the distance is only 75 miles.

A^I advances, fighting for every step of ground, and arrives, after innumerable difficulties and great losses, at Williamsburg, pushing the army B^I before it. B^I has orders to avoid a battle in open field, but to defend with the greatest obstinacy the different works which have been erected to oppose the advance of A^I; it has to retreat without exposing itself to any heavy loss. From Williamsburg it proceeds to Kent, and, arrived there, it retreats to King William instead of Richmond. B^I masks its movement by leaving its rear guard in the presence of A^I; this rear guard has to await an attack of the advanced guard of A^I, and then to retreat on the railway line to Richmond, where it joins the reserve army B^{II}, which is already in a position covered by strong field works at Tunstal.

The object of the rear-guard attack is only to deceive the enemy about the direction the main body has followed, and to draw him at once, by the pursuit he undertakes, in the position he is wished to occupy. It is evident that this rear-guard affair must be conducted with great prudence, so as not to expose the troops to any unnecessary loss.

A^I follows with its whole force, and arrives at Tunstal, in sight of the reserve army B^{II} established there. We may suppose that A^I reaches Tunstal only on the fifth day after its departure from Fort Monroe, although these two places are distant only about two days' march from each other; but we must consider the great difficulties A^I had to contend with, and the fights it had to sustain in its advance.

B^I, by retreating to King William, makes a junction with 50,000 men sent by rail from B, and, amounting now to 100,000 men, they advance against the Richmond railway line, take A^I, which is already engaged with B^{II}, in the flank and rear; they cut it from its lines of communication, and the complete defeat and dispersion of A^I is the consequence of this movement.

In the mean time, A, which is ready for attack, instructed of A^{II}'s advance and B^{I}'s repulse, calculates the moment the

STRATEGY. 33

departure of B's detachment against A^I takes place. It chooses the right moment, and attacks with its superior and concentrated force B's line of defense. This we suppose to take place on the fourth or fifth day after its departure from the Potomac.

B's lines are carried; B is driven back, but not before B^I and B^{II}, and the reinforcement of 50,000 men, had time to complete their victory over A^I, and to advance to the rescue of the retreating B. This fresh army of 130,000 men, confident by their recent victory, joins with B; and B, B^I, and B^{II}, amounting now to about 250,000 men, make an offensive return, forcing, by their great superiority, A to fall back on its own line of defense on the Potomac.

It will take the rebels three days to complete their junction, and the consecutive fights and retreat of A will take some three days more; so that, after about the eleventh day from its departure, A would regain its old quarters.

The brilliant tactical victory achieved by A has been of no use to it, because the strategical victory belonged to its enemy.

The rebels, having once more their own lines of defense, and possessing now a numerical and moral superiority, must pass from a defensive war to an aggressive one; but before showing any further movements of the armies A and B, we will turn to those in the West, and see what is passing there.

The Missouri army is ordered to clear Missouri of the rebels, to advance to the South, to cross the Mississippi, and to occupy New Orleans. This army numbers 100,000 men, and opposed to it are only 80,000; therefore the army A^{IV} advances straight against the rebel army B^{IV}, tries to engage it in a battle, drives it down the Mississippi, and crosses this river as soon as it finds it convenient.

A^{III}, or the Kentucky army, acts in a similar way; it passes the Ohio, attacks the rebel army B^{III}, forces it back, and follows the retreating B^{III} on the line to Nashville. B^{III} and B^{IV} are inferior to A^{III} or A^{IV}; but B^{III} and B^{IV} united are superior to each of the two Union armies; therefore they must try to act on concentric lines, to unite, and to fall upon each of the Union armies separately.

To enable them to act on such a plan, they must hold the principal passages across the Mississippi from Cairo down, and they must complete their interior lines of communication. Besides, A^{III} should be the army first attacked, as by its destruction A^{IV} finds itself isolated, and already separated from the rest of the theater of war.

B^{III} and B^{IV}, in commencing the operations opposed to A^{III} and A^{IV}, engage in no serious battle; they will only fight to stop the advance of A^{III} and A^{IV}, and to arrest their movements. The many rivers that the Union armies are obliged to pass will facilitate the plans of the rebels, who, besides, have space and time enough to act in, as the distance from St. Louis or the North of Kentucky down to the Gulf of Mexico is from 500 to 600 miles, or from 35 to 40 ordinary days' march.

However, B^{III} acts more energetically than B^{IV}; its resistance is stronger and more obstinate, its offensive returns are more frequent; therefore A^{III} advances slower than A^{IV}, whose adversary seems of a more easy disposition; but, arrived at two or three days' march from Memphis, B^{IV} leaves a corps of about 10,000 men opposed to A^{IV} to mask its departure, and advances by forced marches to Memphis. This town, as well as a strong fort which the rebels should have on the right bank of the Mississippi, is occupied by perhaps 10,000 men, troops of the reserve rebel army B^{IV}.

B^{IV} crosses the river at Memphis, and is transported by rail to Decatur, where the greatest part of the reserve army B^V is already stationed. B^{III}, in the mean time, followed by A^{III}, has arrived in the same neighborhood. B^{IV} and B^V united advance against A^{III}'s flank and rear at the time that B^{III} makes a stand in front; A^{III}, attacked by an army just double in number, is completely defeated and dispersed.

The corps of observation which B^{IV} left opposed to A^{IV} has effected in the mean time its retreat, and forms, with the 10,000 men already at Memphis, a body of 20,000 men, whose duty it is to prevent A^{IV} crossing the Mississippi until the defeat of A^{III} is accomplished.

As soon as A^{IV} ascertains that a small corps only opposes it, it can easily imagine what has occurred; if it passes the river, it would come in contact with all the rebel armies united, and its entire destruction would be the consequence; if it remains in the neighborhood of Memphis, the main body of the rebel army will pass on the line to Hickman, and cross the river there, A^{IV} would be cut from its base of operation, and its loss would be certain; it has nothing else to do but retreat at once. The duty of the 20,000 men at Memphis would have been to deceive A^{IV} as long as possible about their real strength, and to make it lose all the time they could, by showing, for instance, dispositions for fighting, or by spreading false rumors, or even by inducing it to cross the Mississippi by a feigned retreat. If, nevertheless, A^{IV} retreats, a body of 10,000 or 15,000 men should follow it and disturb its retreat as much as possible.

The time the execution of those operations will occupy may be calculated as follows: it would take the Missouri army about 14 days to march from St. Louis to Memphis, and the same time for the Kentucky army to go from the Ohio to Decatur.

Considering that the rebels use every obstacle for defense, destroy the bridges, and in general render slow the advance of A^{III} and A^{IV}, we may suppose that it will take A^{IV} about four weeks to reach Memphis, while A^{III} requires five weeks to arrive at Decatur.

The 70,000 men of B^{IV}, who are transported by rail to the junction with B^{III}, will require about five or six days to arrive and concentrate near there, so that the whole operations of the Western armies, from the day they were commenced up to the achievement of the first victory, would take from 30 to 40 days, or three to four times more than those on the Potomac. Here also the rebels must pass to an offensive war, but their action will depend entirely on the operations of the Eastern armies; we must therefore return to them.

We left these armies at the moment A had regained its old line of defense on the Potomac. To justify its future movements, as well as those of the army B, we must refer to the map.

At the beginning of this work, under Strategy, Fig. 1, we have shown the danger of an army occupying a space forming a rectangle, two sides of which belong to us, the third formed by the sea or a neutral country, and the fourth side left as sole retreat. This is exactly the case with the position of the Potomac army. The country, where it is now placed, forms a triangle—one side being formed by the Potomac or the frontier of Virginia, the next by the Chesapeake Bay, and the third by the railway line leading from Harper's Ferry to Baltimore. The two first lines can certainly not be used for lines of retreat by the Union army; and the rebels, by gaining the third side with a superior force, would entirely cut the army A from the Northern States, and force it, in the event of its trying to escape, to open its way with the bayonet. If this should not succeed, the army A would be obliged to surrender.

To execute this plan, which would be similar to the movements of Napoleon at Marengo, Ulm, and Jena, the rebels would have to leave a strong corps of observation opposite to Washington, and with their main force to cross the Potomac above this town, to erect some field works to cover their tête-de-pont in case of retreat, and then advance along the Potomac toward the capital.

The Union army has three lines of conduct left :—

1st. To advance against the rebels, and give open battle.

2d. To await them in Washington, by trying to defend this place.

3d. To try to escape by the road to Baltimore.

In the first case, the condition of the two armies must be taken into consideration.

If the victorious rebels, with 250,000 men, cross the Potomac above the capital, and advance there, and this only two or three days (necessary time for the march) after the retreat and defeat of A, this would only be able to oppose to this army from 180,000 to 200,000 men, disorganized and discouraged, their defeat would be almost certain.

The manœuvre of the rebels would be of much less value, if they were to cross with an army only as strong as that of A, and if the latter had not been previously defeated; however, they might even then act with some advantage, as they would risk little more than their rear guard in case of defeat, and, in the event of a victory, it would be decisive.

If A awaits the arrival of the rebels in Washington, nothing would be gained by it. The only line of communication with the North, being that of Baltimore, would be destroyed by the rebels, and the Union troops in Washington would be soon obliged to surrender in consequence of the want of provisions.

Finally, if A tries to escape on the road to Baltimore, B can easily overtake it, as the distance from this place to Washington is nearly equal to that from Point-of-Rocks to Baltimore. These lines form, with the road from Washington to Point-of-Rocks, a sort of equilateral triangle, and therefore any position which the rebels hold on the last-mentioned line would give them the facility of arriving at the same time as the army A on the opposite side of the Baltimore railway. A would be forced to fight with its rear toward the Chesapeake Bay—that is, with the certainty of destruction in case of defeat.

From what has been said, after the defeat of A the decisive point becomes evidently Point-of-Rocks. The one of the two armies which first occupies it and the passages above this point will evidently be master of Washington.

The two armies, A and B, should therefore make forced

marches to arrive there first; but the distance being somewhat shorter on the left bank of the Potomac, we may suppose that A gains this point before B does, and will defend the passages over the river.

Both armies being exhausted by the different marches and fights, a few days' repose is necessary for them to reorganize; and we may therefore suppose that from A's departure from Washington till B recommences operations on the Upper Potomac, five days more will have elapsed. During those five days A has taken every means to re-establish its army. For this, the 75,000 men of the reserve army A^{II} are called in; 25,000 of the reserve army A^V are called likewise; and the 50,000 men at Port Royal are ordered back, their presence in the rear of a victorious enemy, and so far from the decisive point, being considered unnecessary.

All these measures are taken, but B will evidently not wait to commence operations till A is properly reinforced. At this moment it is decidedly superior in strength, and must try to force the passage across the Potomac above the army A, and act against A's right wing; the latter is thereby obliged to march still higher up the Potomac. A's retreat would be called parallel to the frontier.

Though B advances, A would have the advantage of preventing it gaining ground on Union territory; instead of approaching, it would recede from Northern towns. A is continually reinforced in its retreat by the arrival of fresh troops from the reserve armies A^{II} and A^V.

The Western Virginian army likewise receives orders to retreat, to cross the Ohio in a northern direction, and to unite with A; but, on the other hand, B is also joined by

B^{VII}. A continues its retreat parallel to the frontiers till it arrives on the opposite side of the Ohio, which would take place about 15 or 16 days after its departure from Point-of-Rocks; it is joined by the different reinforcements, and amounts now to 250,000 or even 275,000, to whom the rebels could oppose only about 250,000. A would therefore pass from the defensive to the offensive, and oblige in its turn B to retreat. But B might accept battle in a chosen position, or it might, by some well-combined marches, pass to the Southwest, cross the Ohio below A, and thereby gain a central position between A and the Kentucky army A^{III}.

These different movements of A and B, from the commencement of operations up to the last move of B, have taken 35 or 40 days, at about which time the defeat of A^{III} will also be accomplished, as shown in the preceding pages.

The question now is how the whole rebel force should act.

The war, for them, has become decidedly offensive, and an entirely new plan is to be devised.

The positions of the different armies, at this period of the operations, would be the following:—

A, after leaving Washington well garrisoned, retreated with 150,000 men, was reinforced by 60,000 to 70,000 men from the reserve army A^{II}, besides 25,000 from the reserve army A^{V}, and 25,000 from the Western Virginian army A^{VI}—the whole now forming a total of 260,000 to 270,000 men, who occupy a position on the right bank of the Upper Ohio.

A^{VI} is on its way from Port Royal to New York.

A^{V}, consisting now of only 25,000 men, is on the banks of the Ohio and Mississippi.

A^{IV} is near Memphis, on the right bank of the Mississippi, and commences its retreat.

STRATEGY. 41

B left Manassas with 225,000 men, and was joined by B^{VII} from Western Virginia, and occupies with those 245,000 men a position on the right bank of the Ohio below A.

15,000 men, or B^{VI}, are on their way to join B, as, through the departure of A^{VII} from Port Royal, they have become disposable.

B^{III} and B^{IV} are near Decatur, with 180,000 to 190,000 men, and 20,000 are left at Memphis, opposed to A^{IV}.

It is easy to see that the rebels have the advantage on their side; their armies occupy central positions between those of the Union; their lines of communication are interior, compared with those of the North; and, besides, the army A^{IV} is already placed in such a position that its loss is certain if the rebels make the best use of their time. The difference in the number of men of the armies A and B is too small to give one a decided superiority over the other in an engagement; the tactical arrangements, the moral state of the troops, and many other circumstances would decide who was to be the victor, and then the victory would probably result only in a well-ordered retreat of the defeated party. Considering these different circumstances, the rebels may choose either of two lines of conduct for their plan of offense.

1st. Either B, exciting its troops by the news of the defeat of A^{III}, advances against A before this is reinforced by the Port Royal army, engages, and tries to defeat it—in case of a victory, pursuing A; in case of a defeat, retreating, and making a junction with the advancing reinforcement from B^{III}—or—

2d. B awaits, in a well-chosen and even temporarily fortified position, the attack of A and the arrival of its own reinforcements from Port Royal and Decatur.

B^{III} and B^{IV} have only one step to take—that is, to proceed at once against A^{IV}, and use every means to prevent it escaping to the East.

For this they must reach Cairo before A^{IV} can prevent them, and, having then the passages of the Ohio and Mississippi in their possession, they will act according to circumstances. But 200,000 men are more than necessary to beat 100,000; therefore the army may divide, and act simultaneously on two points—one part, about 140,000 men, may act against A^{IV} and the dispersed army A_V, the other, about 60,000 men, will have to join the army B; their action is offensive, and consequently they must act on divergent lines, to keep the shortest communication for themselves, and to place their own armies between the divided bodies of the enemy.

The larger army of 140,000 men might cross the Mississippi at Hickman, but it is probable that it would arrive too late to cut A^{IV} from its base of operation; and as it must prevent A^{IV} passing the Mississippi, and from retreating to the Eastern States, the passage at Hickman would be a fault, except in the event of its having received the intelligence that A^{IV} was still detained at Memphis.

The rebel army must, therefore, gain the left bank of the Mississippi above the Ohio, and hinder the Union army A^{IV}, by a small force, from crossing, and, by means of several feigned attacks, make good its own passage, and oblige A^{IV} to fight against a superior force.

We will suppose that the rebel army B^{III} follows the plan as just explained, and that the army B awaits its reinforcements. The conduct of the latter might be considered a fault, as an energetic general would not lose this occasion for fighting, considering the excitement of his troops and the discouragement of those of the enemy.

However, A, not being attacked by B, must itself attack, before the latter is reinforced by the armies of the West. B is in a good position; and the superiority of A being only very slight, we cannot suppose that anything decisive will happen in this engagement. However, we will imagine that, in consequence of it, B retreats into the State of Ohio, and parallel to the river, which it crosses at Burlington.

The battle and retreat will take about ten days; so that, arrived at Burlington, B is reinforced by B^{VI}, or 15,000 men, and a detachment from B^{III}, or 40,000—in all, 55,000 men.

It could pass again to the offensive; but A being likewise reinforced by the 50,000 men from Port Royal, no change of importance in respect to their relative strength would take place.

However, A, hearing now of the danger of A^{IV}, will try to make a diversion in its favor or send a strong reinforcement to its support. B should prevent this by acting offensively, by showing dispositions to fight, and by attracting the attention of A as much as possible, so as to give B^{III} time to finish its operations against A^{IV}. We must follow this army, and see how it acts, in order to carry out the plan we have traced.

The rebel army, in the accomplishment of this plan, proceeds with the utmost speed to Paducah; there, or in the neighborhood, it crosses the Ohio. If A^{IV} tries to cross the Mississippi near Cairo, to join with a part of the reserve army A^V, and to retreat at once to the Eastern States, the rebel army advances, and, in forcing it to fight, prevents the execution of this plan. If A^{IV} has followed up its retreat to St. Louis, a small corps only proceeds to Cairo, to destroy or disperse the Union forces near that place, and to make a junction with the 10,000 or 15,000 men from Memphis who have followed the retreat of A^{IV}. They leave a sufficient corps at Cairo to keep this place and the passages across the two rivers, and follow the main body to St. Louis, on the left bank of the river. The rebel army now numbers 150,000 to 160,000 men: 30,000 will be sufficient to prevent A^{IV} passing to the left bank of the Mississippi; those 30,000 men must make some feigned attempts to cross the river, and, with the remaining 120,000 or 125,000 men, B^{III} must endeavor to make good its own passage. To cross in front of A^{IV} would be difficult; but, in trying the passage above St. Louis or the Missouri, it might be easier, and the result would, at all events, be more decisive.

The Mississippi forms a large curve above St. Louis. The Missouri falls in the middle of this curve, forming with the Mississippi below its mouth an angle of about 45° or 50°; above it the rivers run parallel for nearly 30 miles, leaving between them a small neck of land only about five miles in breadth. The Missouri is distant about 25 miles from St. Louis; and if the rebel army passed the two rivers, in one operation it would find itself at once in the rear of the army A^{IV}. This army has in front the Mississippi, the passage of which is closed by 30,000 rebels.

A^{IV} is forced to fight, and, being much inferior in number, would be defeated; the victory would be decisive, as A^{IV} has no line of retreat left.

B^{III} runs no risk in this operation, as, in case of defeat, it

STRATEGY. 45

might retreat directly to the South, or it might again cross the Missouri and Mississippi.

A^{IV}, being defeated, is obliged to surrender. The destruction of the army A^{IV} might be accomplished in about three or four weeks after the defeat of A^{III}, as B^{III} would require only seven or eight days to go, partly by rail, from Decatur to Paducah, the distance not being more than ten ordinary days' march. From this last-named place it might reach St. Louis in a forced march of six or seven days; and if we allow seven or eight more for the completion of operations, this would be sufficient for a very enterprising army and general.

A^{IV} cannot receive any assistance from A, as some time will expire before this one is properly informed of B's intentions, and as, besides, it is too much occupied itself with B. If it takes the direction, with its main body, to Missouri, it will be followed there by B, and will arrive too late; if it sends a strong reinforcement to A^{IV}, this one would probably find B^{III} already established in a central position between itself and the Missouri army; and in the mean time A, being weakened through this detachment, would remain exposed to the now strongly-reinforced B.

After the destruction of A^{IV}, B^{III} should advance and join with B. A cannot prevent their junction, as B^{III} could pass to Paducah, and be transported from there by rail to B.

The relative positions of the two armies would now be—

325,000 Union troops opposed to about 400,000 rebels on the Ohio.

The rebels, with this great force, would advance and take a position on the Ohio and northern boundary of Virginia;

this point being the most offensive of their whole frontier, and by its occupation they effectually separate the Eastern from the Western States.

Here, however, we must observe one thing : operations with 400,000 in one army are impossible ; and the rebels, in order to continue, would be compelled to form several lines of operation, giving a great advantage to the army A, which might now regain by a defensive campaign what could not be obtained by an offensive one.

As this would form an entirely new example, and as the operations already described may give a sufficient idea of strategical movements, we will now leave the present example, and proceed to a criticism of the different operations, so that the reader may well understand why those victories have taken place.

Here I must make some remarks. In the discussion of strategical movements, or, as it is called, making war on the map, the distances are generallly calculated by a certain number of days' march, each from 17 to 20 for ordinary, and about 25 miles, or even more, for extraordinary or forced marches. The distances are mostly taken without the state of the roads being at all considered.

An army in presence of a retreating but always fighting enemy, can scarcely march more than six or ten miles per day, and even sometimes less. The passage of a river generally takes a considerable time, and, before a strong army, becomes nearly impossible.

In the engagements supposed to have taken place, we have made a complete abstraction of all tactical arrangements ; we have always supposed that the strongest in men, and who, according to his force, takes the initiative in the attack, is victorious. This is not always the case in war, although we may assert that well-combined plans, if executed with boldness and daring, have generally a more favorable result than those which do not possess these qualities.

In passing now through the different operations, we conclude—

1st. That the general plan of attack by the Union troops was badly devised : too great a division of forces ; wrong lines of operation.

2d. That, after the failure of the great plan, the Union armies, through the force of circumstances, are more and more conducted to a concentration of all their means, and the adoption of only one line of operation.

3d. That the rebels' plan of defense was based on a co-operation of all their forces on a grand scale, leading to—

Concentration of their forces by the right choice of their lines of operation.

They act concentric in their defense, and always make use of their interior lines.

In their attack they act divergently, and isolate the different Union armies by putting larger armies between them, by keeping up central positions, and by acting with superior force against each isolated Union army.

The campaign of A and A^1 is, in a strategical point of view, lost for them even before it commences.

Their plan of attack may be devised in many different ways ; but the result would be very little changed, as the rebels could at almost any time, no matter what we imagine, transport the mass of their forces successively against A and

A^1; the only difference, perhaps, would be that the ground gained at first by the Union troops would be more; but this is of very little or no consequence, as they would lose it by the following operations of the rebels. If A^1 is much stronger, this would be but of little use, and the case would be the same with A. The fortifications and lines of defense of the rebels should then be stronger too, and more numerous, and the Western armies would have to supply 20,000 or 30,000 men from their contingent to the augmentation of the Richmond army; the final result would be the same.

4th. We see that, by a good choice of accidental lines of operation, we may, even after great disasters, save a whole campaign.

We would call the line of retreat of A parallel to the frontier, or the Potomac, an accidental line of operation; and this retreat should be considered a fine strategical movement, as A, although retreating, prevents B gaining any ground on Union territory, and increases the distance between it and the great Northern capitals, centers of industry and wealth which would have been endangered if it had effected a retreat to the North. (Frederick, in 1757, and Soult, in 1814, executed similar retreats.)

A might, perhaps, have done even better in retreating from Manassas to Winchester, instead of to Washington, if such a course was possible, after the first engagements, forcing it to the retreat, as by such a step it prevents B, at the very outset, from acting against the capital, or dividing it from the North; it remains longer on the enemy's territory, and forces the army B to follow it in the direction of

Winchester; but, on the other hand, it is also more exposed to the attacks of the stronger B.

In neither of these cases, however, can B proceed to Washington, as, in doing so, A would be continually in its rear and on its communications, and A, being now daily reinforced by the reserve army A^{ii}, would soon be enabled to pass again to the offensive, and place B in a similar position to what its own would have been, if it had remained on the line of defense of the Potomac after its defeat.

Whatever A does, the pursuit of B should be undertaken with the greatest energy, and the rebels should try their utmost to force A to fight again, and to prepare it heavy losses; besides, nothing disorganizes a beaten enemy more than a well-conducted pursuit.

On the other hand, A must carefully avoid a general engagement, and act against B only when the result is quite certain, by surprising detachments of it, or by attacking it in the operation of crossing a river, and by destroying that part of B's army which has already passed and cannot be supported by its main army. A should pass again to the offensive only if sufficiently reinforced, so as not to expose itself to entire defeat. It would then be time for B to retreat.

The retreat of B in the direction of Kentucky, and parallel to the Southern frontier, should also be considered as a clever strategical movement,—so much more as it approaches the Western armies, renders a junction with them easy, and can, by means of the Nashville and Richmond railway line, reach the latter town soon enough to prevent an attack by A, if this one had marched in that direction, to take the now only insufficiently occupied fortifications of Manassas.

In the operation of the Missouri army, we see that this army, though acting in conformity with its orders, might have operated very differently to what it did.

Instead of advancing to Memphis, it might have tried to deceive B^{IV}, and, passing the Mississippi near Cairo, force its passage across the Missouri, advance in the direction of A^{III}, to form a junction with this army before B^{IV} could form one with B^{III}; then they might have acted together by trying to obtain a central position between the two rebel armies, the fate of which would then have been easily decided. On the other hand, B^{IV} should have prevented that, in passing the Mississippi at Hickman, and in being transported by rail to the Memphis-Decatur line, and to the junction with B^{III}. In this case, or if in general A^{IV} was suspected of having formed the plan to pass the Mississippi near Cairo, the passages over the Ohio near this place ought to be well guarded by detachments from B^{IV} or B^{V}. The action of B^{III} should have been different from what it was when B^{IV} retreated to Memphis. Instead of opposing A^{III}, it should have retreated as quickly as possible, and have tried to increase the distance by every means between A^{III} and A^{IV}. A^{IV}, in making a junction with A^{III}, cannot use any rail; therefore, if A^{III} has advanced too far, it will pay dearly for its boldness.

If A^{III} and A^{IV} can unite, it will be hardly possible for them to prevent B^{III} and B^{IV} uniting likewise, as they possess the shortest lines, except that B^{III} and B^{IV} make great mistakes—B^{III}, for instance, by engaging itself in a serious fight, in which it is outflanked on one wing and forced from its line of retreat into another direction, or B^{IV} by not making the best use of its time. If, therefore, A^{III} and A^{IV} unite, and B^{III}, B^{IV}, and B^{V} unite too, a battle will follow, but it would probably take place on ground chosen by the rebels, as A^{III} and A^{IV}, in order to obtain their objects— being the destruction of the rebel armies and the occupation of their territory—would be obliged to attack them. The slight numerical superiority, besides the advantage of the ground, would most likely give the rebels the best of the conflict; but, however, the odds would be much more equal than if A^{III} and A^{IV} fought separately against the three rebel armies. Although resulting in a retreat, this would be far from destruction. Returned to the base of operation, they will strengthen themselves by the reserve army A^{V}, and advance again. However, this will show better than anything else that the Union's first plan of operation was wrong, and, even if everything was for the best, it ended by a retreat.

5th. We see, further, in the example, that the rebels made the best use of their time; that speed, and a quick and unrelinquished pursuit of their object, conducted the rebels from victory to victory. If B^{III} and B^{IV}, after defeating A^{III}, had reposed on their laurels, the result would have been that A^{IV} would have retreated to the Eastern States, and the remainder of the reserve army, A^{V}, would have done the same, and, by joining with the great Potomac army, have formed a body equal in strength to all the rebel armies united.

6th. As a general rule, we can also conclude that great

detachments should be avoided, if obliged to act in the rear of much larger armies of the enemy.

With the best will to assign, in the example, a place for the operation of the army at Port Royal, I found it quite impossible to give this army anything like a rôle to play. It was only opposed by a very small force; but, surrounded on all sides by the enemy, it could not leave its base, without the danger of being entirely cut from it. The rebels, with their means of transport, could assemble in a few days a large army, and defeat it. Besides, if the rebels in the North are victorious, this army of 50,000 men would not prevent them being so; and if they are beaten, the result of the war would be decided before its action could commence. Therefore we should reflect well before we embark in such operations; we should consider their enormous cost, and if we will receive an equivalent in the result. Finally, we should keep in view that those expeditions are dependent upon our fleet; that our fleet is neither shell nor storm proof; and, if we are not undisputed masters of all seas, if the fleets at our disposal are not such that one lost could be replaced at once by another, we place the entire safety of our army on the safety of our fleet, and it would therefore depend on the friendship and good-will of our neighbors.

These expeditions might then become of more use to the enemy than to us.

7th. Finally, we conclude that, by the application of the maxims of strategy, we might come victorious out of a struggle with a much stronger enemy, as they conduct us to a concentration of our forces, and to fight only when we can do so with superior against inferior means.

We may say that, in supposing the plan of the Union forces to be the same, the rebels might have effectually defended their territory even with less means—for instance, by opposing the two Western armies with much smaller ones. The main army on the Potomac would then have been transported successively to a junction with the different corps of observation, and, with their assistance, the campaign would have ended in a similar manner. Only the loss of ground at the beginning, by the rebels, would have been greater, and the offensive operations could not have been so energetic as they are supposed in our example. If we give the rebels 400,000, we may suppose them to be distributed as follows: 250,000 on the Potomac, representing B, B^I, B^{II}; the armies B^{III}, B^{IV}, each of 60,000 men; B^V, 10,000 men; B^{VI}, 10,000, and B^{VII}, 10,000 men.

If the attack on the Potomac takes place first, B can easily, as soon as a result there is obtained, send 90,000 men to the West, and, by uniting the different forces in a similar way, as shown in the example, they will still be able to defeat the Union forces one after the other. We may suppose their force to be still less, say 350,000 or 300,000 men: even then they could prevent the advance of the different Northern armies. Their principal lines of defense should be stronger, and their main body should be stationed at Richmond, always ready to be transported to the most endangered part of the theater of war. All armies left opposed to those of the Union are corps of observation; and the more the Northern troops drive those corps back and advance, the more certain would be their final loss, because the farther they have entered the rebel territory, the longer and more difficult will be their retreat, and the more easily they would be overtaken by the rebels' main force and defeated.

GRAND TACTICS.

WE have given, in the preceding chapter, the view of a war in its whole *ensemble*, and we have shown the principles which should guide us in the direction to give our armies.

All our movements and manœuvres, as given in the example, have brought us in the presence of the enemy; and the main object of those movements was, to bring, in the collision, the odds on our side.

It is evidently not enough to have the odds for us; our skill in tactics must be equal to that in strategy.

Our most skillful strategical combinations might prove of very little use, if our enemy, by a very superior tactical arrangement, would wrench the victory, which we have already half won, from our hands.

We must therefore study more closely the arrangement of our troops in fight and battle, see how we may consider an army and a battle; and let us then draw from the definition, as a sort of consequence, the way we should use the one in order to gain the other.

An army represents an accumulation of forces, to be used in destroying the obstacles which another party puts in our way to prevent us attaining our object.

The greater the force, in comparison to the obstacle, the easier this is destroyed.

Marches and manœuvres are the preparations; battle is the act of destruction.

If the preparations have exhausted our forces, we have none left for the destruction, and our own loss might be the consequence.

If the obstacle in our way is too heavy to be removed in one action, we must divide it, and destroy or remove each part of it separately; therefore, with superior forces we should act against each part of the enemy's army, and destroy one after the other. But as the entire obstacle is endowed with life, acts to obtain its own object, and tries its utmost to prevent us attaining ours, it will by every means endeavor to hinder the destruction of one of its parts.

The great art of Tactics is, therefore—

1st. To concentrate such forces on one point of our battle line, that we may destroy or completely remove the enemy's forces opposed to us on that point, before they can be properly reinforced.

2d. To choose such a point for our first action, that the consequence of its success is the destruction or removal of the other parts of the enemy's army.

3d. While we are gaining our first partial victory, to prevent the enemy attaining his own object or reinforcing the part we are beating.

Reflections on these three principal rules will bring us to the following conclusions:—

1st. That we should place, in our tactical arrangements, just as much weight on the employment of our time as we do on our space.

GRAND TACTICS. 57

2d. That the force at our disposal must be divided into parts connected by one organization and acting like one machine, so that we can give each of those parts one of the separate tasks to fulfill, which arise by the arrangement of our time and space on the battle-field.

We have, therefore, first to look to the organization of our armies and the elements composing them, before we can proceed to show their use.

ARMIES.

ELEMENTS COMPOSING THEM, AND THEIR ORGANIZATION.

ARMIES are composed of troops, and troops are composed of armed men.

By the nature of the armament we distinguish **Infantry, Cavalry,** and **Artillery.**

Each of those armed men represents, by his own individual strength as well as by the nature of his arm, a force capable of doing a certain amount of work. The amount of work differs for each of the three arms; their examination will, therefore, be our first object.

INFANTRY.

Infantry forms to-day the mass of our armies; it is composed of men whose principal arm is a gun, on which a bayonet is fixed. The character of the arm shows the nature of the work infantry can produce.

The gun itself is a fire-arm, and its effect can be felt even at a great distance. The force that produces the work is the powder. The right application of the work depends on the skill of the man; therefore, in the management of the fire-arm, skill is more required than strength.

The bayonet, on the other hand, is an arm which can

only be used at close quarters, and in the man-against-man fight. For the management of this arm strength and individual courage are the principal qualities.

By the above definitions, we conclude that the men most distinguished for their skill in fire-arms should be particularly employed for distant fight. Men, on the other hand, distinguished for their great strength and courage, ought to be employed in the man-against-man struggle, and their arm should be the bayonet; this, therefore, conducts us to the adoption of different classes of infantry.

The best marksmen should be taken from the army to form special corps, called sharpshooters, rifles, skirmishers, (*Chasseurs, Jäger.*) Their principal object is distant fight; they have to prepare the action for the mass of our infantry. The strongest men, and those most remarkable for great bravery and courage, and who have seen the longest service, should form what is called a corps of reserve. They should be employed only in the last and most decisive moments, and their great object is to act *en masse* in the struggle at close quarters, and by their strength, bravery, and coolness decide the victory in our favor. The rest of the infantry would be called simply infantry of the line; its object is to form the real line of battle, and to be employed under all circumstances either for skirmishing or for fighting with the bayonet. Here the question arises, if we should arm these three classes of infantry differently, their action, and principally the time of it, being different.

I believe that one and the same caliber and one and the same ammunition should be adopted for all the armies of one and the same country; but I think a difference should be made in the construction of the gun.

All the guns should be rifled, and used with the same ammunition. The sharpshooter's gun should be provided with finer sights; it should be somewhat shorter than that of the infantry, to permit of an easier management. The sharpshooters, once in the engagement, can fire whenever they please, or whenever they have a chance. Each man has time to charge and use his gun with coolness and reflection; therefore to sharpshooters quick-loading guns should not be given; it would induce the men to spend their whole ammunition before they had even arrived to effective ranges.

On the other hand, the reserve and all those troops whose principal task is to fight at close quarters, who act in most parts *en masse*, fire only by order, and, what is still more important, fire nearly always only at the most decisive moment and at short distances, should be provided with guns permitting a quickly-succeeding and unremitting fire.

Infantry acting *en masse* or individually is enabled to fight nearly on every ground, and to surmount, in its advance or retreat, any difficulty which roads or configuration of the country would oppose to it. Infantry can easily make use of cover, and can pass over from eighty to a hundred yards in one minute for great distances; and for small distances, its speed for a time may be even more than doubled. These different qualities have made infantry the principal arm in all well-organized armies.

CAVALRY.

We have seen that Infantry is able to fight at a distance as well as at close quarters; we may say that Cavalry and Artillery form the two extremes of Infantry, and possess each one quality of the Infantry, but in a higher degree. Cavalry is only fit for fighting in close battle; when exposed to distant fight, its loss is certain. Artillery, on the other hand, is only fit for distant fight, and close quarters is its death.

The arms of the horse soldier are his sword and horse; fire-arms are also used, but they are more to inspire confidence or to give signals, than of real use on the battle-field.

Cavalry, therefore, acts only by the muscular strength of the parts composing it; being formed of two parts, each endowed with force, the man and the horse, we can use either the strength of the man or that of the horse, or both combined. In other words, cavalry may be used only for the speed of the horse, as in ordnance service, or in fight where speed and shock of the horse, the bravery and strength of the man, find their consecutive employment. This would lead us to the adoption of different kinds of cavalry. Light cavalry, with the duties of outposts, pickets, foraging parties, for expeditions in the enemy's flank and rear, and for reconnoitering parties, etc.,—here speed is the principal requisition; daring and the capacity for fighting should evidently be found also, but we do not require strength and power in such a degree as we do for heavy and medium cavalry. This should act by its force and shock; speed is needed only for short times.

The perfection of fire-arms has made cavalry, and principally heavy cavalry, lose much of its importance; and it is probable that one good medium, or even only light cavalry, will, in a short time, be exclusively used. Cavalry, although quicker than infantry, cannot be used on all ground. Its speed can, for a time, be double that of infantry.

Cavalry amounts, in most of the European armies, to one-sixth or one-fifth of the infantry; but it is probable that the next wars will reduce this number.

ARTILLERY.

In Infantry and Cavalry individuals form the composing elements; in Artillery it is the arm.

The arm of Field Artillery is a gun reposing on a carriage drawn by four to eight horses, and served by ten to twenty men; it fires shots from 6 to 12 pounds, and shells up to 24 pounds. The object of artillery is distant fight; therefore, a powerful and precise fire is of the first importance. The fire is directed against movable objects; besides, its effects increase or decrease according to the distance; therefore the guns should possess facility of movement in an equally high degree.

The last two years have, by the introduction of rifled guns, worked such changes in the construction as well as the employment of this arm, that I will perhaps be allowed to say a few more words concerning it, than I did of the other two arms—so much more, as all the advantages which may be derived from a right choice of rifled guns are generally not yet fully understood. In passing in review the whole history of gunnery, we find, from the day of the invention of cannon, the manifest desire to have powerful guns and to have manageable ones. To the heaviest 24 and 32 pounders on the most awkward carriages, used together with 2 and 3 pounders dragged by the men, we see succeed lighter 24-pounders on more manageable carriages, used together with horse artillery and light 6-pounders. With the mobility of armies we see increase the mobility of guns in general. 24-pounders are replaced by 12 and 18 pounders; horse artillery, light 6 and 4 pounders, were made still lighter than before. Carriages, caissons, and the whole organization of artillery were arranged to permit of all calibers having a greater facility of manœuvre. This was the state in which we find artillery only some few years ago. Powerful artillery was represented by 12-pounders, heavy and long guns, and by 24 and 32 pounder howitzers. Manageable artillery found its representatives in the light 6-pounder gun and 12-pounder howitzer of horse and foot artillery. In comparing the different times, we see that, with the improvement of the *materiel* and the many succeeding inventions, the calibers of the light and heavy artillery approach nearer each other; however, up to two or three years ago, most countries had still four or five different calibers, and consequently as many different artillery organizations, in their armies. In large armies simplification became a necessity. The first step was taken by the present Emperor of the French, in whose army all guns and howitzers were replaced by one light 12-pounder gun firing shot and shell, and uniting powerful fire to great mobility. In its fire it was inferior to the long and heavy 12-pounder, but superior to it by its mobility; in this last quality it was somewhat inferior to the light 6-pounder, but at the same time surpassing this one by the power of its fire. This gun was constructed on the principle that a heavy projectile fired with a small charge is preferable to a light one fired with a heavy charge. The application of this principle soon conducted to the construction of rifled guns; and with their introduction we may say that artillery has entered an entirely new phase. From a rifled gun an elongated projectile, weighing more than the round bullet of the same diameter, is fired, with the same or even a smaller charge of powder than the last one. The initial velocity of the elongated projectile will be smaller than that of the bullet; but its ranges will be greater at equal elevation, *already* at short distances, because it more easily overcomes by its greater weight the resistance of the air. The initial velocity of the projectile being small, that of the recoil of the gun will be small too. We therefore conclude that by rifling guns we can fire a heavier projectile from a lighter gun, which means that we can unite in one and the same gun great power of fire with great mobility. The great art of the artilleryman is to choose from the infinity of variations of rifled guns the right one—that is, a gun possessing the highest degree of mobility joined to *only* the requisite quantity of power of fire. The lightest gun that can be found producing this required amount of power of fire will, therefore, be the best, and the model for field artillery. A 9-pound shell fired with precision up to 3000 yards is as much as we should demand of a field gun. Few countries permit ranges over 2500 or 3000 yards; if above these distances, scarcely anything can be discerned: 2500 to 3000 yards is, therefore, the limit for the ranges; and as regards the weight of the projectile, we can only choose between 12-pound shells and those of less weight; heavier shells would conduct us to too heavy an artillery. The inferior limit of an effective shell is from 9 to 10 pounds; below this weight, the shell would have too small a diameter. The ranges of 12-pound and 9 to 10 pound shells are little different; the question will, therefore, arise, if the greater bursting effect of the 12-pounder will make up for the quarter more weight, or, at equal weight, the quarter-less shells, that we must carry with us in the field, besides the difference in the weight of the guns and the more or less mobility which would be the consequence. I think the question should be answered in the negative, and has been answered so by nearly all European artilleries; the consequence was that, in nearly all European armies, rifled 4-pounders, firing a 9 to 10 pound shell, were introduced, as the *only* field guns, and we may say that the construction of this gun was the solution of the greatest problem of artillery since the invention of powder. The Armstrong, Whitworth, and many other rifled guns, corresponding in their weight more to the smooth-bored 6-pounders, all those beautiful weapons may be said to be of faulty construction as field guns; they possess an excess of power, but are far from having the mobility of the rifled 4-pounder. This rifled gun is drawn by only four horses, and served by only six men. The Prussian 4-pounder gun is, however, in nearly every respect superior to the French one. Being equally light, its *ranges*, and principally its *precision*, are much greater. The introduction of those guns has wonderfully simplified the organization of field artillery : but one caliber throughout the army, but one kind of ammunition, but one organization as mounted artillery, reduction of costs and losses by the employment of less horses and men, multiplied action by its great mobility, and great effect by its powerful and precise fire. Firing but shells, with infinitely more precision up to 3000 yards than the smooth-bored 12-pounders could fire their shots at 1500, it replaces advantageously guns and howitzers. Considering the standard of the science of artillery, we may say that, to-day, any field gun requiring more than four horses, to execute with ease its manœuvring on any kind of ground, is of faulty construction, and possesses an excess of power to the detriment of mobility. It is very possible that the introduction of these light guns will conduct to an augmentation of the arm in general, and at the same time bring about a reduction of cavalry.

The number of guns now employed is about three for every 1000 soldiers; it will probably come to four or five. With new and inexperienced soldiers, the number of guns should be greater than with old and tried troops. In speaking of the use of the three arms in battle, I will say a few more words concerning the management of this new artillery.

ORGANIZATION.

We have seen in the preceding chapters what are the elements composing an army. These elements must be joined with an organization to permit of their simultaneous action.

Their simultaneous action is only possible by submitting them to one will; therefore an army is commanded by one person, and must be commanded by one person only, and not by two or more.

The orders of the commander must be executed by the elements composing the army. The commander cannot give orders for each element separately; therefore our elements should be formed into a certain number of bodies, and their commanders *only* should receive the orders from the commander-in-chief.

The number of those under-commanders one chief can attend to is restricted. Experience proves that the number should not be less than three or four, and not more than eight or ten. An army of 200,000 men, for instance, might, according to this, be divided into eight parts, each part numbering 25,000 men. For these 25,000 men we come to the same conclusion that we did for the whole army; subdivisions must be made, not less than three or four, and not more than eight or ten. These subdivisions must be again divided, and so on till we come to the unit of evolution—that is, one body composed of elements—which is not any more divided in the evolutions, as given in the small tactics of each arm. These divisions have received names, which are: **Army corps**, a body of 20,000 to 50,000 men, making part of a large army; **division**, a body from 10,000 to 20,000 men; **brigâde**, from 4000 to 10,000 men; the brigade is composed of regiments, regiments of battalions, battalions of companies, squadrons, and batteries, and these of platoons, sections, etc.

A regiment is composed only of elements of the same

arm; it can be of infantry, cavalry, or artillery. A brigade can be composed of infantry or cavalry; it can also be composed of the three arms together. A division is ordinarily composed of two arms, infantry or cavalry joined with artillery, but it can likewise be provided with the three arms. The army corps is always composed of the three arms, and forms in itself a small army.

The battalion of infantry, squadron of cavalry, and battery of artillery form what is called a tactical unit. In speaking of the force of an army, it is generally given by the number of battalions, squadrons, or batteries. Their strength varies in the different armies. In the European armies, a battalion amounts to from 600 to 1300 men; squadrons, from 80 to 200 horses; and batteries, from 4 to 12 guns. Too strong a battalion is too difficult to move, and too small a one too soon used up; it is the same with squadrons; very strong batteries are subject to be too often divided. For infantry, battalions of 800 to 1000 men; for cavalry, squadrons from 100 to 150 horses; for artillery, batteries from 6 to 8 guns, are, however, the numbers generally used. Regiments of infantry are composed of 2 to 4 battalions. Regiments of cavalry, from 4 to 10 squadrons. Regiments of artillery, from 4 to 12 batteries. The brigade has generally 6 battalions; the division, 2 or 3 brigades; and the army corps, 2 or 3 divisions.

The organization of an army is different in nearly every country, and it is hardly possible to find one that is faultless. The bodies forming the immediate subdivisions of an army should be provided with the three arms, and form

GRAND TACTICS.

small armies by themselves; they should be able to fight independently of the main body.

The number of brigades in these small armies is of importance. If we form a line of battle, 3 brigades would be preferable to 2, as we would be able to have one on each wing and one in the center; but we must have a reserve, and, besides, we might be compelled to make detachments: this would give us 2 brigades more, and would then lead us to an army corps composed of 5 brigades instead of 3. In treating of marches, we shall see that the number 5 is also the most convenient in the arrangement for marching in several columns.

The formation of these brigades should be different, each one having different tasks to fulfill. The brigade for detachment would be, in many cases, obliged to keep up a fight independently of the other 4 brigades; it should, therefore, be provided with the three arms, and principally with the elements permitting a well-sustained distant fight, as in many cases it would have to contend with superior numbers, whose advance it would have to arrest or retard. The three brigades forming the line of battle require no cavalry, as they can be provided with this arm from the reserve; they should each have a battery. The reserve brigade, acting only in the last extremity, should be composed of the best infantry regiments, besides all the cavalry and reserve artillery. This would give for the first brigade, which we will call advanced guard brigade, a composition of 4 battalions of infantry, 2 battalions of rifles, 2 batteries, and 4 squadrons; for each of the 3 brigades of the line, 4 battalions of infantry, 1 battalion of rifles, and

1 battery; for the brigade of reserve, 4 battalions of infantry, 6 squadrons, and 6 batteries.

The more the organization of an army is complete, the more the command is facilitated; the order given at the head passes in a few moments through the whole army, and all the parts of this great mass work like one machine; but the command has only put all those forces to work; the work itself must be assigned beforehand. Besides, the machine must be kept in the best possible order; in other words, an army must be provided with ammunition and provisions; if it marches, the roads must be pointed out to the chief of every division or army corps, the time of the different movements determined, the places where rivers are to be passed shown, the means for crossing the rivers provided, orders for marching given, the place for each army corps in battle assigned, the time of action, the moment for the arrival of the different bodies, the lines of advance or retreat must be fixed in general and for each of the smaller parts in particular.

It is quite evident that the commander-in-chief of an army cannot attend to all these details; therefore he has another general under him, who is called the chief of the general staff, whose duties are to render possible the ideas and orders of the general-in-chief, and to see that those orders are properly carried out. Besides the above-mentioned duties of the staff, there are others which consist in a thorough study of the theater of the war and the providing of the most complete and correct maps, the working out of the general plan of campaign, the special plans of the battles, the receiving and giving the orders of the general-in-chief, etc. etc. The commander of each army corps has his special staff.

In treating of the three arms separately, we have spoken of their proportions in an army; those proportions change much, according to the country and the length of the war. It becomes, therefore, one of the principal studies of a general, to always choose such ground for his actions, where he can make the best use of the arm in which he is superior, and where he can best spare the arm in which he is deficient. Large plains are best adapted for the action of heavy artillery and cavalry; hilly country, light artillery and infantry; covered ground, infantry and sharpshooters. Too small a quantity of artillery is dangerous, because our own troops, being too much exposed to the enemy's fire, and without the means of returning his ravages, would become demoralized. To new troops a strong artillery is of great advantage; after a check, it covers their retreat, and gives them time to reassemble; it well prepares their advance. Too small a body of cavalry forces us into narrow limits, prevents us from well surveying the surrounding country and from gathering information concerning the enemy; besides, cavalry alone can turn a defeat into a rout.

Generally speaking, the strength of an army depends on its number, the right proportion of the three arms, the confidence of the troops in their leader, and the general character of the men who compose the army.

NORMAL ARRANGEMENT OF TROOPS IN BATTLE.

Now that we know the elements and how they are united, we must see how they are to be disposed, to execute the order of their commander for a simultaneous or successive action. Men, we have seen, represent forces capable of doing a certain amount of work in a certain length of time. The work done, exhaustion will follow for another length of time, till the strength of the men is re-established by food and repose. In an engagement, the exhaustion of our forces arises from several causes—the fatigue of the men, the using up of the ammunition, and their exposure to the destroying work of the enemy; this last cause acts on the *number* of our forces, and is even of more importance than the two others. Therefore we conclude that, if all our men commence work at the same time, and all act simultaneously, their action will be short and their exhaustion will be simultaneous; if, on the other hand, they act but in small parties, and one party after the other, their work will be done successively, their action will be long, and total exhaustion will only follow after a great length of time.

If we dispose all our men in one line, $a\ b$, Fig. 9, parallel to the line of the enemy $m\ n$, each man will represent one of the forces, f. We see that all those forces act simultaneously, but also that they are all exposed to the work of the forces f' of the enemy's line $m\ n$. The time of the action will therefore be short,

GRAND TACTICS. 73

and ab will be soon exhausted. If, on the other hand, we dispose all our forces one behind the other, Fig. 10, and make them act against $m\ n$, one force after the other will act, the work will be done successively, the time of the action will be long, and the exhaustion of the entire force will only follow after a greater length of time.

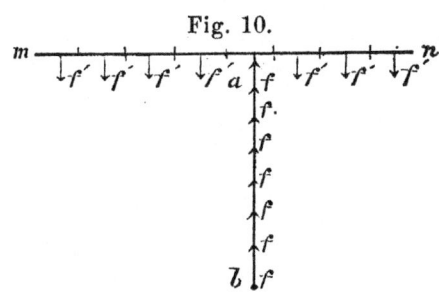

Fig. 10.

The representation for simultaneous action will, therefore, be the arrangement of our men in line parallel, and that of a successive action in line perpendicular, to that of the enemy. Applied to a battalion, this means for the first disposition in line deployed, for the second in columns.

Experience has given limits to the extension of lines and the depth of columns. Lines may be used in open and close order. In open order we see the skirmishers act; and if they do not form a regular line, their arrangement bears, at all events, the character, as it permits their simultaneous action. Arranged in close order, two or three ranks are chosen in preference to a single rank. Columns may be of different depths—those which have the necessary depth for fighting, and those which are only used in marching to overcome the difficulties of the ground more easily. From eight to ten ranks, one behind the other, are sufficient to give a column the desired quality of a longer sustained fight. More than eight or ten ranks would only be an unnecessary accumulation of force which would never be required for action.

7*

Whatever we adopt, the line or the column, they will be both used up in the engagement; the length of time only will be different. If, therefore, to prevent our whole force being exhausted too quickly, we divide it into two parts, leaving one behind the other out of the enemy's reach, we will be enabled at any time to bring fresh troops in the conflict, and, by choosing the right moment for action—that is, when the enemy, by the struggle with our first force, is already weakened and in a state of confusion—those fresh troops will evidently have the best of it. This conducts to the arrangement of two or more lines of battle, one behind the other.

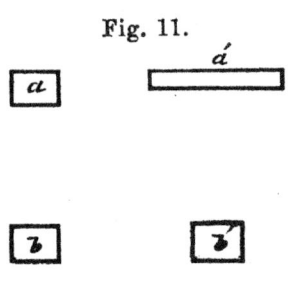

Fig. 11.

If, for instance, a and a', Fig. 11, represent each a battalion, a arranged in column and a' in line, two other battalions, b and b' should be arranged behind them. To advance, being formed in line, is difficult; and, as b and b' must advance at the right moment, they are both arranged in columns.

To permit the action of b and b', an interval must be left between a and a' through which b and b' can advance. If

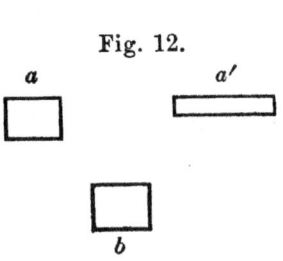

Fig. 12.

b and b' are in straight line behind a and a', their advance through the interval will be more difficult; besides, if a and a' retreated in disorder, they might involve b and b'; we may, therefore, arrange b and b' in the intervals of a and a', Fig. 12.

GRAND TACTICS.

The length of the intervals will depend on our intention to fight formed in line or in columns. If we suppose that a, a', a'', and b, b', b'' represent battalions, Fig. 13, they may all have to act in columns.

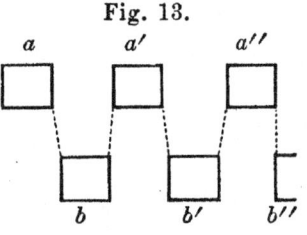
Fig. 13.

The distance from the center of a to the center of a', Fig. 14, must, then, be equal to the front of a and b both formed in column. If a, a', a'' have to form in line, and b, b',

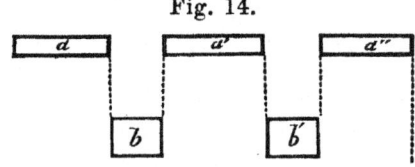
Fig. 14.

b'' remain in column, the distance from center to center of a and a' must be equal to the front of a formed in line and b in column.

Finally, if a, a', a'' a'' are formed in line, Fig. 15, and the interval should be such that b, after advancing,

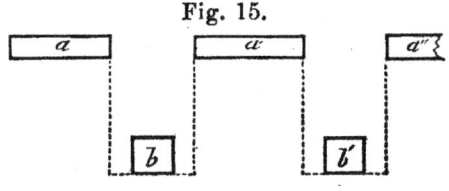
Fig. 15.

could form in line too, the distance from center to center of a and a' must be equal to the front of a and b both formed in line.

We may, according to circumstances, employ any of the three arrangements, as well as considerations of different nature may oblige us to increase still more the distance between a, a', a''.

But the arrangement of the enemy's troops is similar to ours; the moment our second line of battle advances against his first victorious one, his second line of battle, consisting of fresh troops, advances against ours; therefore a third line would be necessary. As, however, on many points our two lines might prove sufficient, and as we do not know on which point the third line of battle might be required, we form it in one mass called reserve; this mass is placed near the center of our whole line of battle, and will act, or send reinforcements to the endangered parts only of our front line. As soon as its action is finished in that one part, it returns to its first position. If we have a point of great importance to defend, or if we wish to make a very vigorous attack on any particular point there, we may arrange more than two lines of battle.

We do the same with troops very apt to get into confusion. Cavalry, more easily disordered, should always be arranged in more lines of battle than infantry. Artillery, on the other hand, never fighting individually, cannot get into disorder, and requires, therefore, but one line.

There remains to be shown the average number of men disposed on every yard of the front line of battle. It is easy to see that the number of troops will be different according to the distance between the centers of a, a', a'', and we have seen that those distances vary much. It is admitted that from 2 to 5 men, for each yard of the front, is a low number, from 6 to 8 an average, and above 8 a high number. We must, however, observe that an order of battle may not be deep, even if there are 8 or more men for every yard of the front. The meaning of a deep order of battle is, that a long fight can be kept up and continually supplied with fresh troops pouring in from the rear.

The number of men for every yard of the front line de-

GRAND TACTICS. 77

pends greatly on the ground. Covered ground requires less troops, and admits of less men for every yard of front. The defense always requires less than the attack, and especially if favored by the ground. Therefore the distribution of forces may be very different near the different parts of the front. Near the main attack, from 10 to 15 men may be placed for every yard, while in other places, perhaps 2 or 3 could only be disposed. The number also varies with the total strength of the army; a small army will have less men for every yard of the front than a larger one.

In nearly every country normal battle formations have been adopted; those formations varying with the organization of the armies, it would be much too long to give even a part of them, as there are so many variations; but as, in the last chapter, I have given an organization for an army corps, I will now show how this army might be arranged, leaving the ground entirely out of the question. We have supposed, in the organization, that the army corps had 5 brigades, 1 advanced guard, 3 of the line, and 1 of reserve. The advanced guard may be called upon to fight independently of the remaining portion of the other body, or they might fight together, the advanced guard being the first attacked. I will give several plates showing how the troops might be arranged in the different cases. Those normal battle formations may be of great advantage when we have not much time for reflection—if attacked, for instance, on a march. The arrangement of the troops in those normal orders, as given in the plates, will show that, in fact, the troops are disposed in four lines of battle instead of two. The skirmishers form the first line; they act in open order, and their action is simultaneous; their exhaustion soon follows. The second line finds its employment principally in the distant fight, but at effective ranges; from this it passes to the fight at close quarters; there it is relieved and sustained by the third line; and if this line is not sufficient, the fourth one, or reserve, must join its action with the three preceding ones.

As a general rule, however, for all these arrangements, without considering whether the space be large or small, we may say that a great portion of it should be kept in reserve; in the first line, only the number of troops just necessary should be placed.

EXPLANATION OF PLATE FIRST.

This plate shows the normal battle formation for a brigade, composed of 2 battalions of rifles, 4 battalions of the line, 4 squadrons, and 2 batteries.

Having ordinarily to resist a superior number, the movement of which it has to arrest for some time, or at least to retard, it must develop a great quantity of fire; this is attained by bringing the 2 battalions of rifles in the skirmisher line, and by dividing the battalions of the line in half battalions, and disposing them as shown in the plate; the reserve, which remains in hand, is quite sufficient to resist any sudden attack on one particular point of the line.

1 and 2 are the two rifle battalions.

3 and 3, 4 and 4, 5 and 5, 6 and 6 are the four battalions of the line.

Order of battle for the advanced guard brigade

1 Sharpshooter battalion
2 "
3 Battalion of the line
4 "   "   "   "
5 "   "   "   "
6 "   "   "   "
I Squadron
II "
III "
IV "

Plate I

0   100   200   300   400 Yards

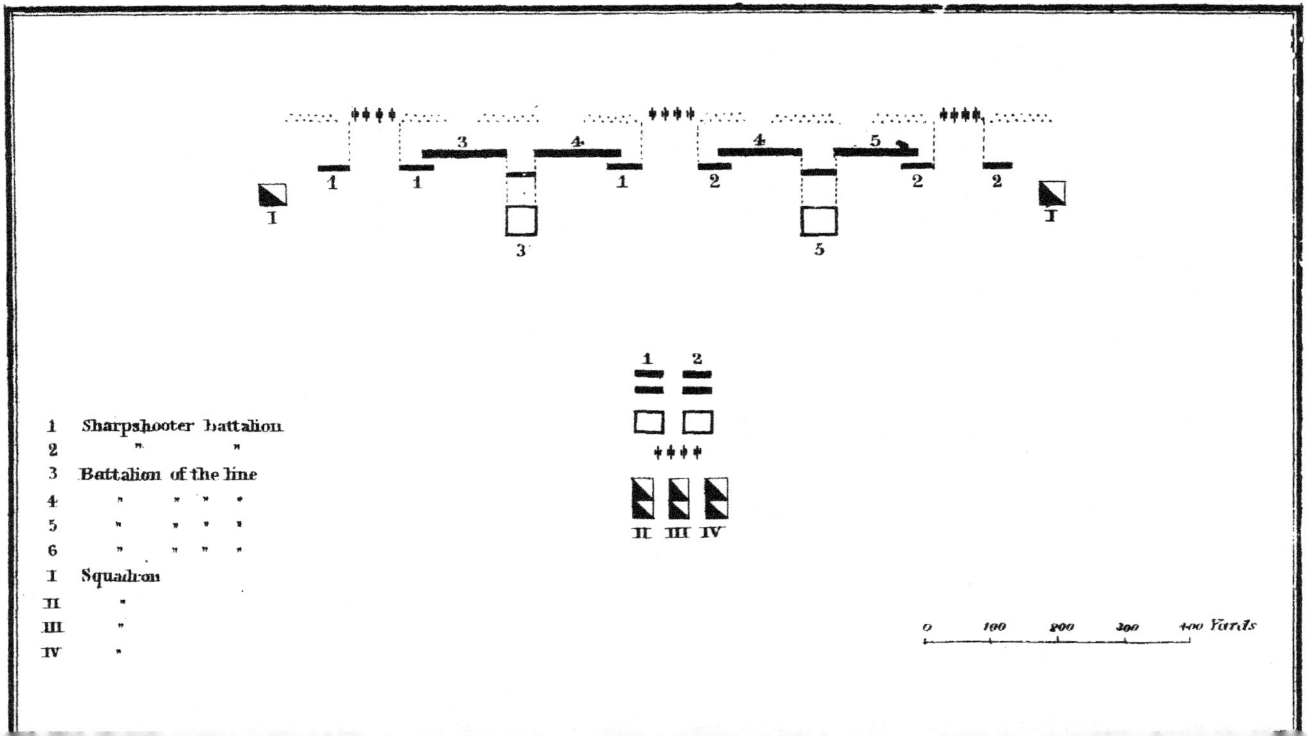

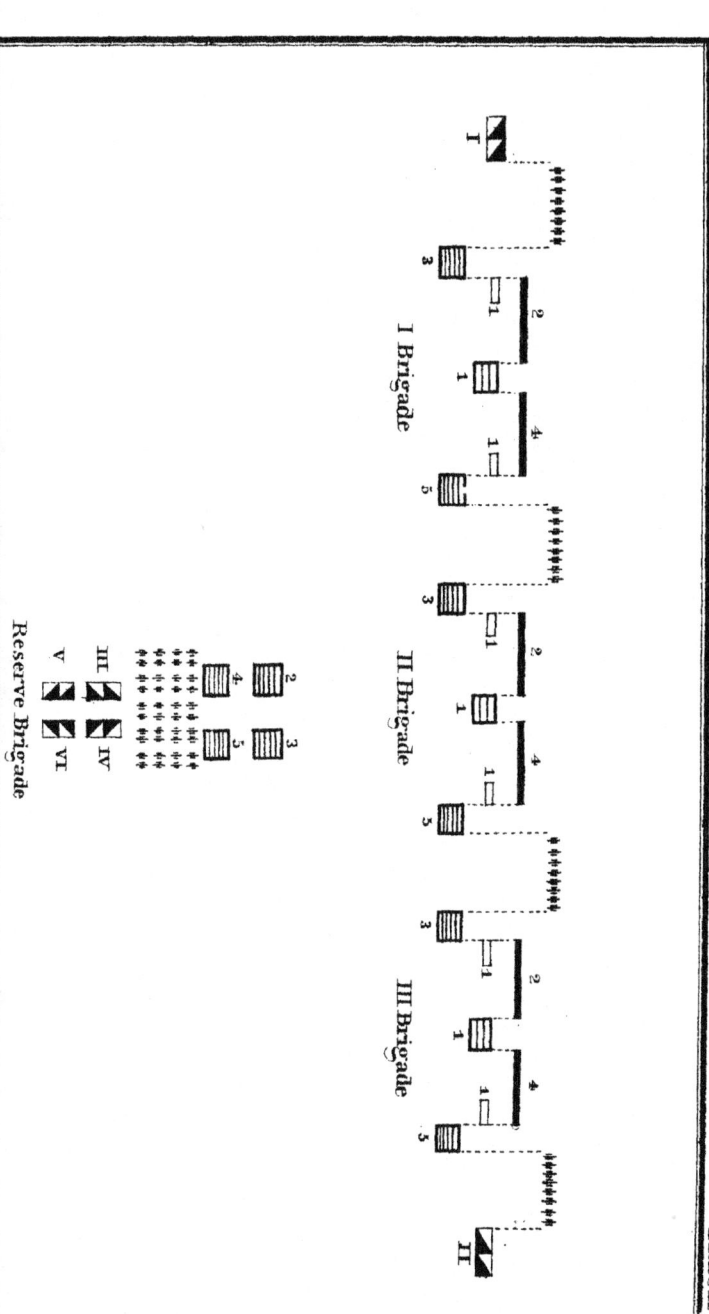

I., II., III., IV. are the four squadrons of cavalry.

Of the 2 batteries, 1 battery and a half are in position, one half remains as reserve.

The rifles, in case of advance, form in the intervals in columns of company.

EXPLANATION OF PLATE SECOND.

This is the order of battle for a whole army corps; if the advanced guard brigade is present, it is kept in reserve, as shown in Plate IV. I., 1, 1 are the battalions of rifles; they form in the intervals between 2 and 4, and send out the skirmishers whenever they are required.

2, 3, 4, and 5 are the battalions of the line.

I., II., III., IV., V., and VI. are the six squadrons. Only four batteries are in line, 5 are kept in reserve.

BATTLES, FIGHTS, SKIRMISHES, Etc.

We distinguish between battles, fights, and skirmishes.

Battles are fought between the main bodies of two armies.

Fights are the rencounters between the larger portions of the main body.

Skirmishes are the rencounters of two small bodies or advanced guards of larger bodies, without the intention on either side to engage in any serious fight.

If the parts of a great army are so strong that they form in themselves armies, any serious engagement with a similar corps of the enemy may be called a battle.

On the other hand, a rencounter between two main bodies may bear only the character of a fight, in consequence of the small number of troops engaged, the insignificant result of the affair, and the wish on both sides, or on one only, to avoid a battle.

We have seen in the foregoing chapters that battles are the consequence of our strategical arrangements and movements. If we understood by our strategical plan the way to direct our concentrated forces against smaller bodies of the enemy, which we could easily defeat, a whole campaign might end in a series of fights. But if the enemy has as well calculated his movements as we have, an engagement of the main bodies will probably take place, which, in consequence of the results, will be called a decisive or drawn battle. In this engagement, one or both parties may have acted aggressively. A battle can, therefore, as well as a whole campaign, be aggressive, defensive, or of the offensive defense. The whole nature of the war, as well as our preceding strategical arrangements, will most probably decide which of the two parties is to be the attacking one. If we have gained the strategical victory—if, for instance, our manœuvres have conducted us on the communications of the enemy, we might await his attack in the position chosen by us; our object being not merely to repulse the enemy from our position, but to defeat and destroy him, we would be conducted to a battle bearing the character of an offensive defense.

If, on the other hand, the enemy's army stands in our way, and prevents us attaining our object, we would naturally become the attacking party; and finally, if we were inferior to it in number, and our only object consisted in the defense of one of its passages, we might be conducted to a purely defensive battle.

PURELY DEFENSIVE BATTLES.

We can only determine upon fighting a purely defensive battle in case of a great inferiority to the enemy; we must then choose such a position as will make up for the deficiency of men. This position should prevent the enemy from developing any larger force than our own. It should present many obstacles, to make the enemy lose time in trying to surmount them; this time that we gain should be employed in acting against his already engaged, separated, and inferior forces by our superior fire. But we should not choose too strong a position, because the enemy would then try to turn it; and there exists scarcely any position which cannot be turned.

In general, there is little to be said on purely defensive battles; their whole art consists in making the right use of the ground. They can never be decisive, as the only thing we could do would be to repulse the enemy, but not defeat him; they would retard, but never prevent, the final result: the enemy, repulsed on one point, would choose another, and force us to fight in a less favorable position. Those battles may, however, be advantageously chosen, if their main object is to retard the enemy's progress, and to gain the necessary time for assembling our principal forces on the really decisive point; but then those battles have more the character of a subordinate fight than that of a main action.

DEFENSIVE BATTLES WITH OFFENSIVE RETURNS.

We are conducted to such battles if the whole nature of the war is defensive for us; if we have been the defensive party in the strategical struggle; or, finally, if we have gained such a strategical victory over the enemy that we oblige him to attack us. The arrangement of defensive battle will always depend more or less on the nature of the ground; by choosing our own ground, we will evidently make the best use of it. The relation between the configuration of the ground and our arrangement will, however, vary much with the object we have in view.

We may compare the general who fights a defensive battle with offensive return to a swordsman waiting to parry the thrust of his adversary and to follow it by a thrust of his own, or to the more consummate swordsman who feigns to be off his guard in order to induce his adversary to make a certain thrust, which he parries and follows by a deadly blow. This little illustration may be applied in the following manner: 1st. To await the enemy's attack in a chosen and strong position; to proceed ourselves to the attack only at the moment he enters our lines or that we have repulsed him. 2d. To await the enemy's attack in order to bring his forces in such a relative position to our own that his defeat or his destruction is inevitable. In this case, we do not even await his attack, but commence our own as soon as his troops have arrived in the required positions. In the first case, only defeat, in the second, total destruction, may be the consequence. The first, where the decision takes place, will be in our own lines; in the second, it will be in advance of them. The general battle arrangements and orders of battle, as well as many other considerations, will be the same as those of offensive battles; they will, therefore, be treated in the next chapter. I will give two examples—the plans of the battles of Austerlitz and Talavera—for the better understanding of battles of the offensive defense. The battle of Talavera is an illustration of the first, and that of Austerlitz of the second case.

OFFENSIVE BATTLES.

We are conducted to such battles if the nature of the war is aggressive; or if the enemy opposes the attainment of our strategical object; or if we are forced by the manœuvres of the enemy; and, finally, if by a wrong movement he exposes his army, or parts of it, to certain defeat. In an offensive battle two things may occur :—

1st. That the enemy awaits us in a chosen position.
2d. That we meet him unexpectedly on the march.

In the second case the general dispositions are the same as in the first, with the exception that we have no time for making any premeditated arrangements : a few words, therefore, will suffice to explain this second case, as all general arrangements will be spoken of in treating of the first one. The enemy, in finding us unexpectedly in his way, will probably be as much astonished as ourselves; therefore the one of the two who acts first with the greatest energy and coolness, and, principally, who has studied beforehand the entire configuration of the country, the principal roads, courses of rivers, mountains, distances of villages, extension of woods, etc. etc., and who has chosen the best order for marching and the best roads for the direction of his troops, will have the advantage on his side; he will at once find the important point where to direct his efforts, to concentrate his troops; and, being victorious there, he may attach little importance to secondary points. In unexpected battles the genius of a general will show itself more than in any other.

In the first case, we suppose that the enemy awaits us in a position chosen by himself. Our first care should be to obtain a thorough knowledge of the ground, as well as the strength of the enemy's forces and the position they occupy on that ground. One will be obtained by being provided with good topographical maps; the other we must ascertain through spies, prisoners, deserters from the enemy, reconnoitering parties, and even by preparatory attacks. The information we gather concerning the enemy, and a knowledge of the ground he occupies, will partly tell us the object he has in view. But, before devising our plans, we should divide the battle-field into three zones—right, left, and center; and, to prevent us undertaking any dangerous enterprise, we should force ourselves to answer all questions which may present themselves in reflecting on the intentions and relative positions of the two armies; such questions might be, for instance, as follows :—

1st. What is the enemy's object?

2d. In which of the three zones has he concentrated his forces for the attainment of his object?

3d. What is the probable amount of those forces?

4th. What is the probable amount of forces in the two other zones?

5th. How can he act, from his position, on our communications, lines of retreat, flanks, and rear?

6th. Which of the three zones, by the configuration of the ground, is the easiest to attack, and which is the easiest to defend?

7th. How are the enemy's forces distributed in accordance with the configuration of the ground?

8th. In which of the three zones ought we to act for the speediest attainment of our strategical object?

9th. In which of the three zones will we the soonest obtain an easy and partial victory?

10th. Will this zone permit us following up that partial victory, or will this victory, by the configuration of the ground, remain isolated?

11th. If the zone in which lies our strategical advantage is separated from the zone which would give us the first partial victory, which of the two zones should we choose?

12th. If the pursuit of the first partial victory is impossible in the zone where it is the easiest obtained, which other zone should we choose?

13th. When we find the point on which our first victory should take place, what time would probably elapse before that victory could be gained? what amount of forces should we employ?

14th. How long would it take the enemy to send assistance from the supposed position of his reserve to the threatened point?

15th. How could we prevent the enemy sending assistance to this point?

16th. What would be the required force to prevent the enemy obtaining his own object, while we are gaining our first partial victory?

We see by these questions and the answers we would be obliged to give—

1st. That the different points of the battle-field present very different degrees of importance.

2d. That the time, in our plan, must be just as much considered as our space. For instance, if we leave the enemy time to send his reserve, and perhaps one or two other divisions which he could spare, to the threatened point, our anticipated victory might end with defeat.

We conclude, therefore, that we must distinguish on our battle-field five different objects :—

1st. The main attack in the zone we have chosen for our first partial victory.

2d. The feigned attack, if we think one necessary to draw the enemy's forces on this point.

3d. The preventing of the enemy obtaining his own object for the time we need to complete our first partial victory.

4th. The engagement of the enemy's remaining forces, to prevent their employment on other parts of the battle-field.

5th. The demonstration : to engage the enemy to make a detachment, to divide his forces in order to prevent a supposed attack or to keep free his line of retreat.

The Main Attack.

In the choice of the zone for the main attack, we should be guided by the consideration that the first partial victory must be obtained quickly, but at the same time the easy pursuit of this victory must be possible. The attack itself should be conducted with the greatest precision and energy.

The introduction should be short.

Arrived at very effective ranges, the fire of artillery as well as that of small arms should be overwhelming. To the fire the struggle at close quarters should succeed ; there we should concentrate our best infantry and cavalry. The principal thing in the main attack is that we should develop a decided and overpowering superiority in all the three arms over the enemy.

Feint Attack.

If we think it necessary to make another attack, we should choose such a point for it that the enemy would not consider a main attack impossible on that point. As we have seldom many troops to spare for these attacks, they should be directed against the weakest parts of the enemy, his flank or rear.

The direction and forces should, however, be such that the enemy must reinforce the point where the attack takes place. If it is successful, the victorious corps should at once pursue its victory, and by this assist the main attack. The time for this attack is generally before, and the distance of it should be as great as possible from, the main attack.

As regards its action, the introduction of the fight might be longer, and likewise the fight at effective ranges, as it is not executed with such imposing forces; but this should not lessen the energy. The advance from effective ranges should be firm and steady up to the last moment, when the struggle at close quarters begins. The attack, if repulsed, should be repeated with still more energy.

Number Three.

While those two attacks take place, we must prevent the enemy attaining his object; this can only be done by opposing him, in the zone which he has chosen for the execution of it, with a body of such strength that he is unable to obtain it before we can complete our first partial victory. This corps that we oppose to him should act principally by its fire. It should form large reserves, in infantry as well as artillery, which should be used at the last and most decisive moment only; it should make the best use of its cavalry—act in such a way that the enemy, who advances supposing but little resistance before him, is at once and unexpectedly assailed by fresh troops, superior fire, and a cavalry ready to charge him at the least sign of disorder. This corps, in other words, has to play on a small scale the rôle of a battle of an offensive defense.

Number Four.

To engage with the enemy in order to prevent him making use of his different corps. The real object being more to threaten than to act, a strong fire should be kept up on these points; the corps having this task to fulfill should use its reserve, and principally that of artillery; it should deceive the enemy on its strength by its multiplied fire, and make him believe that it would pass at any moment to a serious attack.

Number Five.

The object of the demonstration is to force the enemy to make a large detachment. If we send a detachment on the communications of the enemy, he would be obliged himself to make a detachment even larger than ours, in order to keep clear his line of retreat. The detachment made by the enemy, the object of the demonstration is obtained.

The figures will explain more fully what has been said:—

If $a\,b$, Fig. 16, is the enemy's line of battle, if our main attack is directed against the center by the corps m, we might oppose the two wings only by small bodies, n and o, as explained under Number Four.

In the mean time n and o are driven back to n' and o' by the two wings of the enemy; we have been victorious in the center, have advanced to m', and force by this both wings to retreat. In this figure we distinguish three actions—the main attack in the center, and the keeping of the wings in their positions by n and o, and at the same time the preventing of the enemy to attain his object.

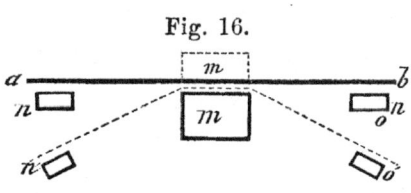

Fig. 16.

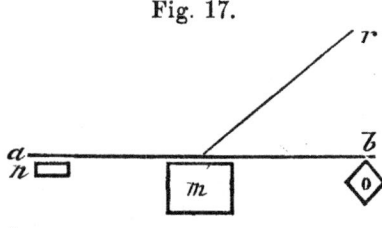

Fig. 17.

Or, if $a\,b$ is the enemy's line of battle, Fig. 17, we may dispose a main attack in m, and a feint attack in o, with the order to proceed to r on the communications of the enemy; n would be a small corps only to keep the right wing of the enemy in its place. In this figure we have four actions—those enumerated under 1st, 2d, 3d, and 4th.

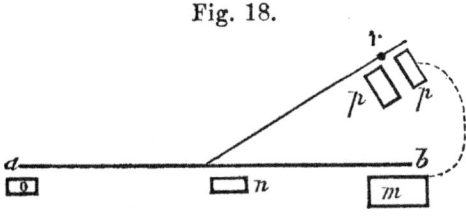

Fig. 18.

Or, if $a\,b$ is the enemy's line of battle, Fig. 18, if we send a corps p to r on his communications, he is obliged to oppose to us a larger detachment, p', to force us from his line of retreat. This would be a demonstration.

In uniting the different possible combinations, we come to the following general orders of battles:—

1st. The line of battle forms a straight line and is parallel to that of the enemy; this line can be—

    a. Without reinforcement on any point, Fig. 19.

Fig. 19.

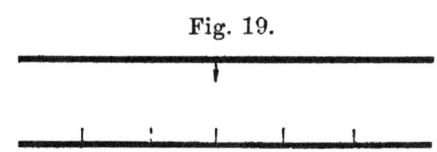

b. Reinforced in one of the three zones, Fig. 20.

Fig. 20.

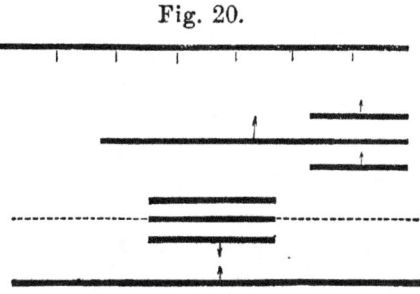

c. Reinforced in two of the three zones, Fig. 21.

Fig. 21.

2d. The line of battle is a straight line, but inclined to that of the enemy. It has—

    a. One point of attack, properly called an oblique line of battle, Figs. 22, 23.

Fig. 22.

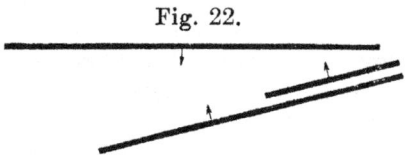

Fig. 23.

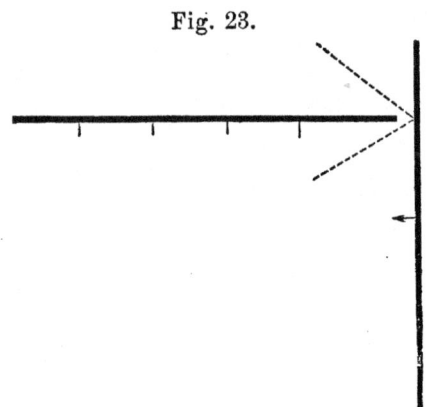

b. Two points of attack, Fig. 24.

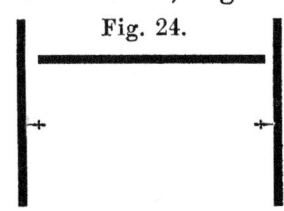

Fig. 24.

In *a* and *b*, the angles can be 90 or under 90 degrees.

3d. The line of battle is a broken one formed in echelons.

a. One point of attack, Fig. 25.

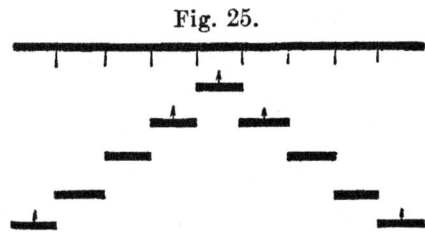

Fig. 25.

b. Two points of attack, Fig. 26.

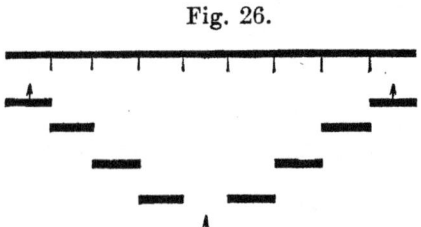

Fig. 26.

GRAND TACTICS.   93

4th. The line of battle is a straight one, but forms a crotchet on one flank, Fig. 27.

Fig. 27.

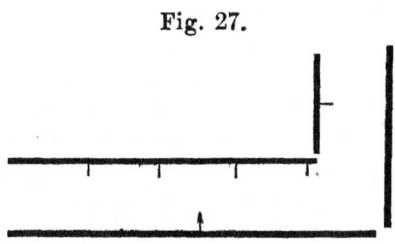

5th. The line of battle is a curve.
  a. Concave, Fig. 28.

Fig. 28.

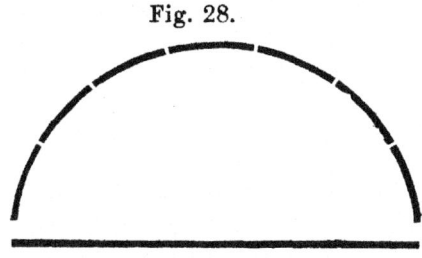

b. Convex, Fig. 29.

Fig. 29.

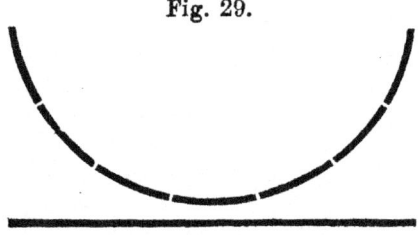

The first order of battle, being a straight line without any reinforcement, would be the arrangement, as the French would say, of a *sabreur*. This battle would represent the primitive state of the art of war.

However, there is one case in which we would adopt it,

and even be obliged to do so—that is, after gaining the strategical victory, and already on the enemy's line of communication; then we might have no reason to reinforce any one part; but as, in such a case, we would be obliged to have very strong reserves, they would represent a reinforcement of the center, or of the point threatened by the enemy.

Wing or reinforced center attacks are much more used and more convenient than simply parallel orders. The battle of Austerlitz, given as an example of a defensive battle, may be also taken for the example of one with a reinforced center.

Attacks reinforced on the two wings, or center and one wing, can be undertaken only in case of superiority. I will give two examples—the battle of the Alma, with two reinforced wings, and the battle of Wagram, with one wing and center reinforced.

The orders of battle under No. 2, making angles with the enemy's line, are principally used by an inferior force against a superior one. The plan of the battle of Leuthen, one of the most remarkable, will explain this oblique order of battle.

Double attacks of oblique or perpendicular lines should only be attempted when the aggressor is of very great superiority.

Attacks in echelons may be used against an enemy who cannot easily move from his position, and can therefore undertake no concentric fire on the first echelon, as would be the case in the attack of an entrenched camp.

Lines of battle with crotchets may be used by the aggressor; for the party attacked they are always dangerous, the corner being exposed to a concentric fire. The battle of Prague, fought by Frederick II. against the Austrians, will be the example for this order of battle.

Convex lines of battle were used at Leipsic and on different other occasions; we are often obliged to use them after the passage of a river. They offer one great disadvantage; if broken at one point, the enemy finds himself at once in the rear of his adversary's whole formation of battle.

Concave lines of battle have sometimes been used. Hannibal's formation at Cunna was such. They should, however, only be adopted according to circumstances; if, for instance, the enemy's position forces us to it, or if this formation is the consequence of the advancing fight, the center giving way and the two wings approaching.

Such is said to have been the plan of the Austrians in the battle of Solferino, 1859.

EXAMPLES.

EXAMPLE OF BATTLE WITH TWO WINGS REINFORCED.

BATTLE OF THE ALMA.

Fought the 20th September, 1854, between the Russians and the allied English, French, and Turks.

Armies of the Allies.

TURKS.	—Division of	Sulliman Pacha . . .	6000
FRENCH.	"	General Bosquet . . .	6750
	"	General Canrobert . .	6750
	"	Prince Napoleon . . .	6750
	"	General Forey	6750
ENGLISH.	"	Sir Lacy Evans . . .	5250
	"	Brown	5250
	"	Richard England . . .	5250
	"	the Guards	5250
	"	Cathcart	5250
	"	Cavalry	800
		Total	61,000

With 136 guns, consisting principally of 9 and 12 pounders.

The Russian army consisted of—

Infantry	30,000
Cavalry	3000
Artillery	2000
Total	35,000

With 96 guns, part of which were light guns.

On the 19th September the allies formed in line of battle as follows:—

Right wing—General Bosquet, Sulliman Pacha.
Center—General Canrobert, Prince Napoleon.
As reserve—General Forey.
Left wing—the whole English army.
In first line—Sir Lacy Evans and Brown.
In second line—Richard England and Guards.
In reserve—Cathcart and Cavalry.

The Russian army had taken a defensive position on the heights of the left bank of the Alma. (See plan.) The allies, after having reconnoitered this position, decided to attack it on the 20th September, and made the following arrangements:—

1st. The division of Bosquet, with the division of Sulliman Pacha, to advance at 5.30 A.M. of the 20th; to pass the Alma near the sea, ascend the heights on the left bank of the river, to turn the left flank of the Russians, and proceed to the attack.

2d. The left wing, consisting of the whole English army, to advance at 6 A.M., march against the right wing of the Russians, and to try to turn it.

3d. The center of the army, consisting of the divisions of Canrobert and Prince Napoleon and Forey, to advance at 7 o'clock to attack the Russian center.

This plan was, by different mistakes, only half executed. The whole of the French army followed the division of Bosquet, and formed their line of battle with their rear toward the sea. The English closed near them; and so it happened that the Russian right wing was not attacked at all, and, after a fight of from two to three hours, the Russian army found itself in the position R on the plan, and the French and English in A F.

The Russians retreated in the best order, and unmolested by the enemy. We may well ask if 61,000 French and English could not have done better than to force 35,000 Russians to a well-ordered retreat.

The dispositions of the Russian commander, Prince Menschikoff, were made in the expectation of a main attack on the road to Burluk; this road was well swept by a battery of four 32-pounders; and in case the regiment Borodino (15th) was driven back, the advancing columns of the enemy would have been assailed on all sides by such a fire that their retreat would have been very probable. His plan of battle was of an offensive defense, but becoming offensive only at the moment the enemy entered his own lines. His front was about 7000 yards long, and counted, therefore, five men for every yard of the front, which number was quite sufficient, considering the nature of the ground. His position is given in the small plan I have subjoined; having the sea on his left and the allies in front, he can only retreat in the direction of his rear or right wing; any manœuvre against his right wing, placing him between the forces of the allies and the sea, will therefore force him to leave his position or expose himself to total destruction.

We distinguish in the plan of the allies three different actions:—

1st. The main attack against the Russian right wing, executed with 27,000 men.

2d. The feint attack against the flank and rear of the Russian left wing, 13,000 men.

3d. Engagement in front, to keep the Russian forces in their place, and to prevent them acting elsewhere, 14,000 men.

The French reserve of about 7000 men could act wherever its presence was required.

For the main attack nearly the half of the allied army was disposed, and this was quite right, only the order was rather vague and uncertain in saying that the English should try to turn the Russian right wing. It should have said that the English were to force, at whatever price, the extreme right wing of the Russians, and to proceed at once against their lines of retreat. This manœuvre ought to have been the part of the French, whose army was better organized for rapid manœuvres than the English, which still kept to its old system of lines as used by Wellington.

The main attack was to commence half an hour after the feint attack. The feint attack was to be executed by 13,000 men, and was to be the first act of hostility. What must be the result of this attack? The Russians, seeing a body nearly as strong as the half of their army appear on their left flank, will form a crotchet with their left wing, and, being assailed at nearly the same moment by the English on their right flank, will dispose of the center troops not yet attacked to oppose the English; and, seeing the danger of their position being turned and attacked at the same time, will commence a retrograde movement on their lines of retreat, which are still open. The French center, therefore, if the arrangements are well executed, having for object to keep the Russian troops in their position, arrives too late.

The same insignificant result—the well-ordered retreat of the Russians—was in fact obtained by the allies' wrong execution of their plan, only with greater loss on both sides. The Russian right wing not being attacked, Menschikoff could very well defend himself as long as he pleased; his communications and retreat in the interior remained always free, and, even if defeated, there was little danger for him, as the allies had no cavalry to pursue him.

If the allies had well reasoned the objects of the two armies, the plan, and probably the result also, would have been different. Menschikoff expected an attack in front; this was very evident by his whole position and arrangements; therefore he should have been left in this belief; he should have been first attacked in front, to deceive him on the real point of attack. The disposition of the allies might, therefore, have been—

1st. The English army, 27,000, to attack the Russian center and left wing in front, and to commence its action at 5 A.M.

2d. The division of Sulliman Pacha, 6000 men, to advance at 5.30, and pass the Alma near the sea, proceed against the Russian left wing, draw the attention of the Russians to it, and force them to make a detachment in this direction.

3d. The division of Bosquet, 6750 men, to attack the Russian right wing at 5.30.

4th. The divisions of Canrobert, Napoleon and Forey, to advance at 6 o'clock, when the whole Russian force is completely engaged, turn the Russian right wing, attack the regiment Uglitz, and establish itself on the Russian lines of retreat.

With 21,000 French on their line of retreat, to which the Russians had not one man to oppose, with 33,000 English and French in front, and 6000 Turks on their left flank, all attacking at the same time and all in communication, it

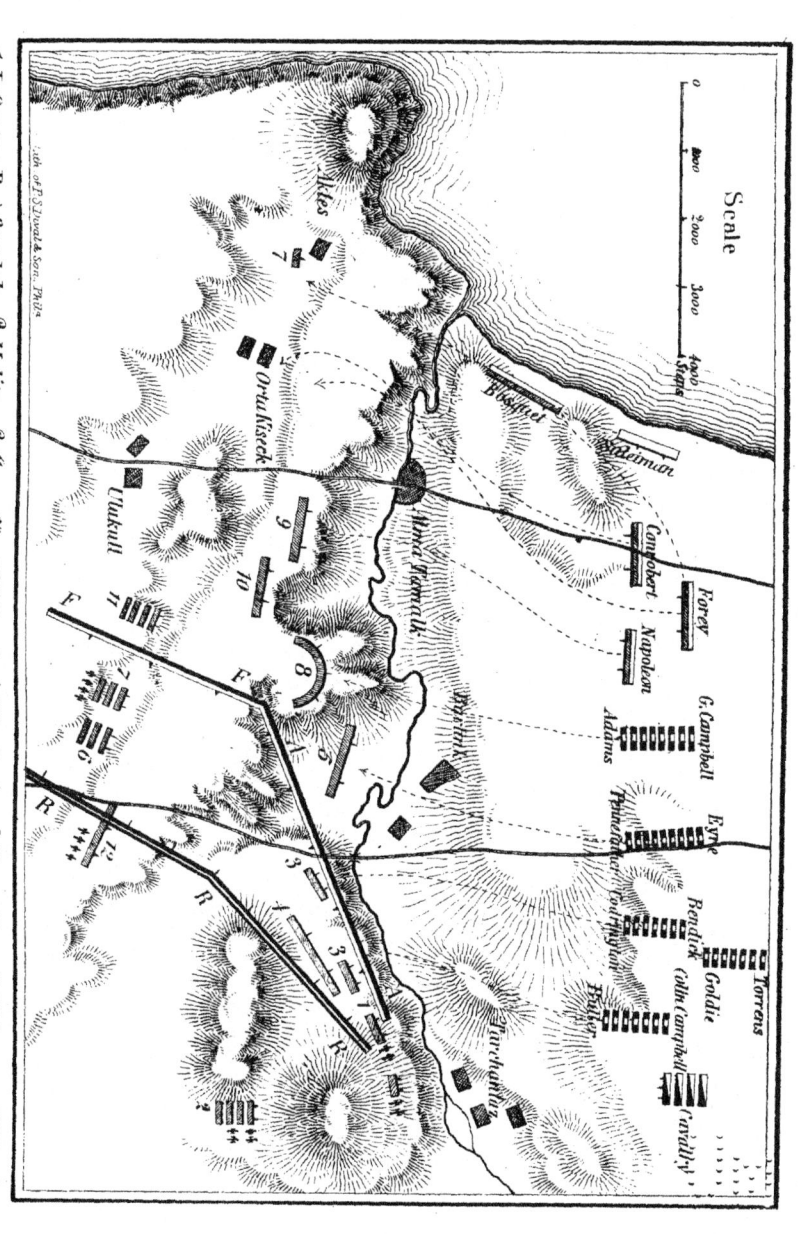

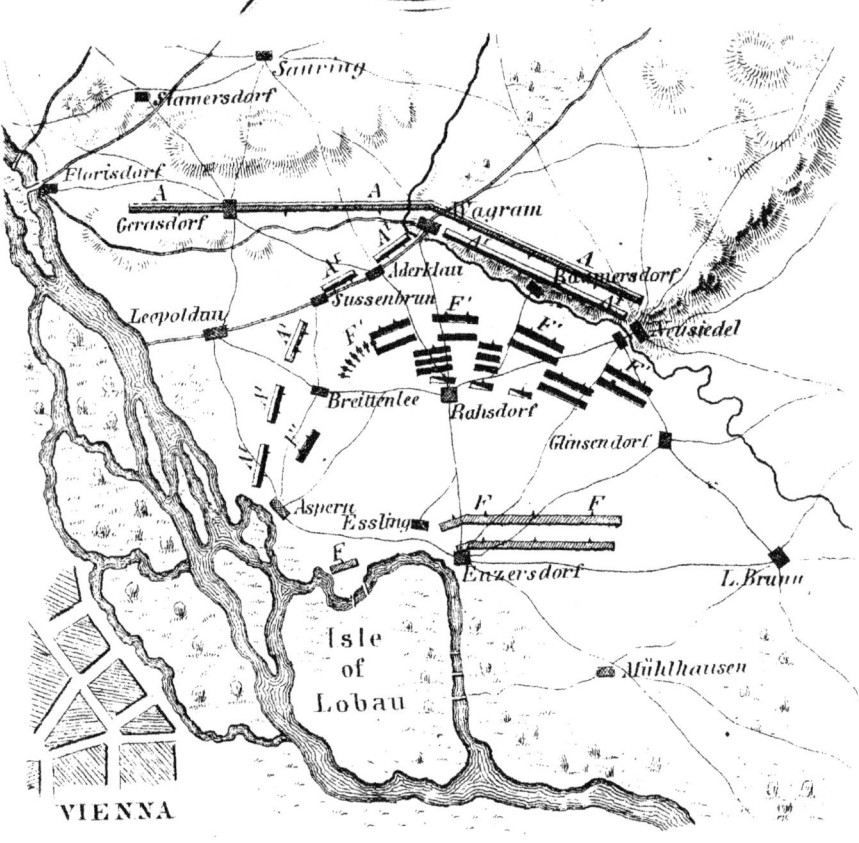

Battle of WAGRAM July 6. 1809.

- ▬ First position of the French.
- ▬   „   „   „   „ Austrians.
- ▬ Second position of the French.
- ▬   „   „   „   „ Austrians.

is probable that the Russians would have been obliged to surrender. Sebastopol would have been the easy trophy of the victors, as it was without garrison at the time of the battle, after which only it was supplied from the army of Menschikoff.

EXAMPLE OF BATTLE WITH CENTER AND ONE WING REINFORCED.

BATTLE OF WAGRAM, JULY 6, 1809.

The army of Napoleon amounted to 150,000 combatants, that of the Archduke Charles to 120,000.

On the nights of the 4th and 5th of July the French crossed the Danube, and took on the 5th the position F F; on the 6th they advanced in the position F' F' F'. In consequence of this, the Austrians proceeded to the attack by taking the position A A. Their right wing, consisting of 50,000 men, advanced to the attack of Napoleon's left wing, which he had refused; this consisted of one division, commanded by General Boudet. This left for the Austrian center and left wing but 70,000 men, against which Napoleon had concentrated nearly twice that number. The length of his front for center and left wing was about 11,000 yards, the accumulation of forces amounting, therefore, to from 11 to 12 men for every yard.

Massenas's corps, with Bernadotte's, is opposite to Aderklaa.

Oudinot's corps, with Lannes's, is opposite to Baumersdorf.

Davoust, with his corps, is opposite to Neusiedel.

Eugene, Wrede, and Marmont are in advance of Rahsdorf, in third and fourth lines of battle.

On the left of the center, a battery of 100 guns forms the communication between the center and the left wing.

This battle can also serve as an example of a convex and concave order of battle; it shows well the danger of the convex order.

If the Austrians force the left wing of the French, they find themselves at once in rear of the whole army. In this case, however, this operation could not be executed with the necessary energy, as their total inferiority was too great; and, while they were attacking the French left wing, their own left wing and center were treated in the roughest manner. The Austrian left wing was outflanked by Davoust, and the retreat of their whole army was the consequence.

The retreat was, however, effected in good order; and the loss on both sides was nearly equal, amounting to about 20,000 killed and wounded for each party.

EXAMPLE OF AN OBLIQUE ORDER OF BATTLE.

BATTLE OF LEUTHEN, DECEMBER 5, 1757.

The army of Frederick II., King of Prussia, commanded by the Duke of Bevern, had been defeated, near Breslau, by Field Marshal Daun, commander of the Austrian army, amounting to about 86,000 men. The king, hearing of this disaster after the victorious battle of Rosbach, hastened, with about 15,000 men, to Silesia, where he made a junction with the remaining portion of the army, commanded by the Duke of Bevern. His whole force amounted now to about 30,000

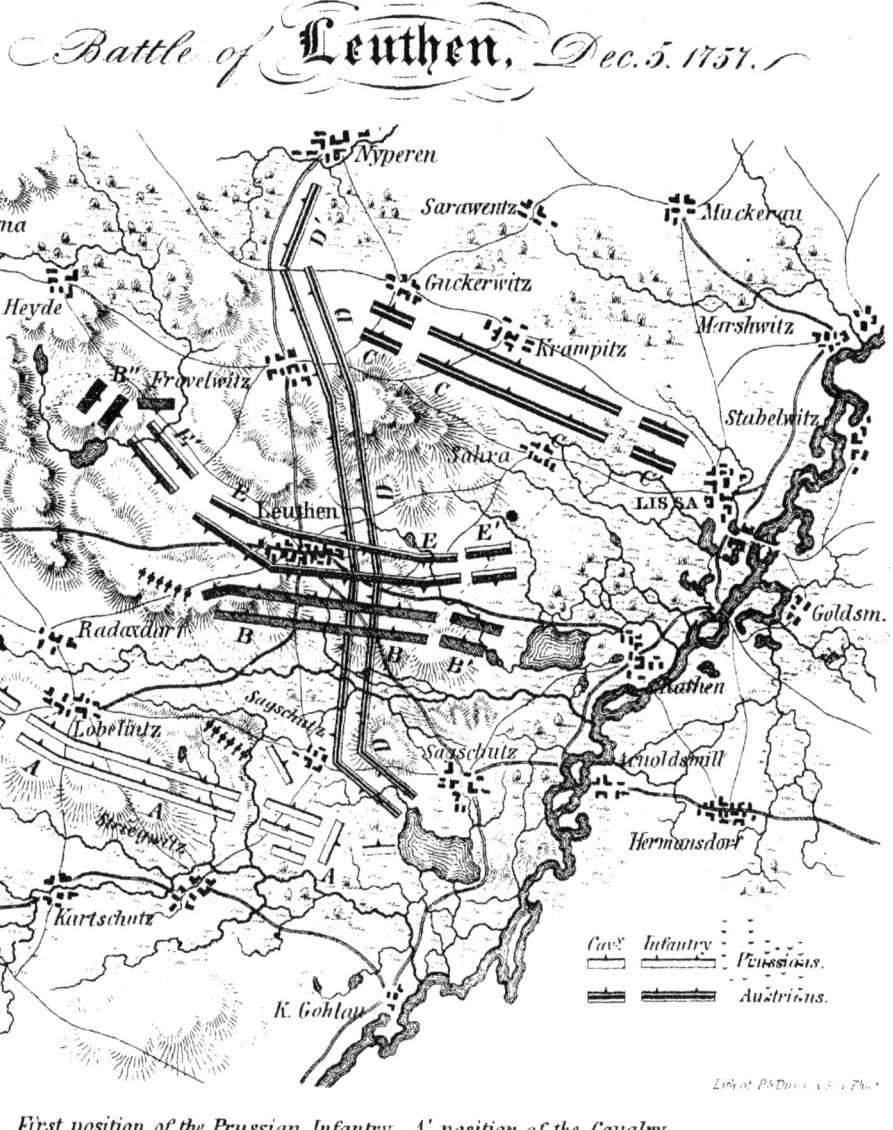

_First position of the Prussian Infantry. A'. position of the Cavalry.
Second „ „ „ „ B'. position of the Cavalry on the right wing.
position of the Cavalry on the left wing. C & C'. positions of the Prussians after the Battle.
First position of the Austrians. E. second position of the Austrians.
E'. Austrian Cavalry.

men. Frederick addresses himself to his soldiers, telling them of the dangerous position of the Prussian monarchy, and excites them to the highest pitch.

In the mean time the great Austrian army takes its position at Leuthen, near Breslau, awaiting the king to give battle. Frederick arrives near the Austrian position, orders a feint attack near Frovelitz by his advanced guard, in order to deceive the enemy on the real point of attack, and in the mean while he brings his army in the position A A, as shown in the plan. The Austrian left wing is attacked by a superior force, and is defeated. The army of the king advances, continually defeating and outflanking the Austrians, and arrives at B, where the rest of the Austrian army is formed in a new line of battle; their right wing is battered by a heavy battery, which had already taken their whole line in echarpe. The Prussian cavalry of the left wing charges the cavalry of the Austrian right wing in flank and rear, and drives it entirely from the field of battle; it then returns, and attacks the Austrian right wing in rear, and completely defeats it. The Austrian left wing, in the mean time being outflanked, is obliged to retreat. C C is the position of the Prussians after the battle.

By this victory the king regained his provinces in Silesia. The Austrian loss amounted to nearly 50,000 men, including 32,000 prisoners.

In this battle we distinguish three different actions — the main attack; a very short and insignificant feint attack, bearing more the character of a demonstration; and, finally, we see, by the inclined position of the king's army, a part of the Austrian front continually kept in position, in the expectation of being attacked.

In this battle we see better than in any other the greatest principle of war brought in action — to always act with concentrated and superior forces against inferior forces.

The first partial victory conducted the king to a series of small victories, all of which were obtained by a superior force against a weaker one. By the oblique movement of Frederick, the ends of the Austrian lines were continually outflanked, and attacked in front, rear, and flank, thereby rendering all resistance impossible. One-half of the Austrian army was defeated before the other half could change its position and form a new front. The left wing of this new front was already in great disorder before it could be formed, and the right was so promptly attacked by the Prussians that it had no time to form. If the king, instead of making an oblique movement, had moved straight down the Austrian line, his own right wing would have been easily outflanked. Frederick, at the battle of Kollin, had proposed a similar plan of attack; but a mistake of one of his generals prevented its execution.

EXAMPLE OF BATTLE WHERE ONE WING FORMS A CROTCHET.

BATTLE OF PRAGUE, MAY 18, 1757.

The Austrian army, amounting to about 80,000 men, had taken a position near Prague; this position, if well defended, it was scarcely possible to force—one wing bearing toward the Moldau, and the front and right wing covered by a small river and marshes. Only four small passages were left to the Prussians to attack the Austrian army. The Prussians,

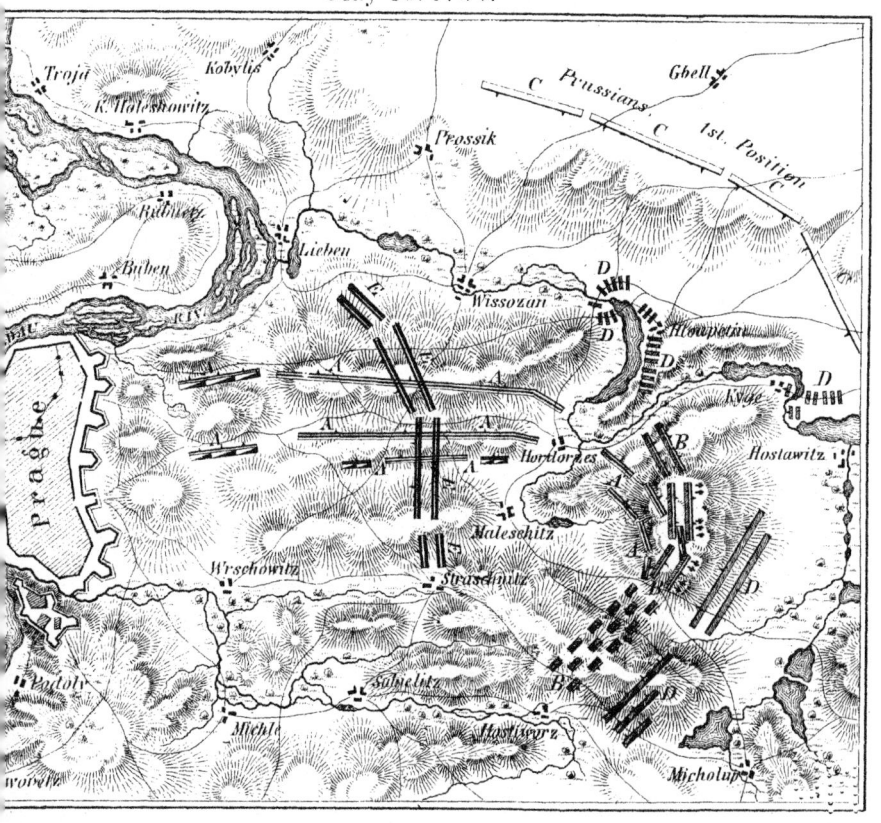

BATTLE OF PRAGUE,
May 18. 1757.

A.A. First Position of the Austrians; their right wing changes in B.B.
D.D. Second position of the Prussians; E.E. Position of the Prussians after the Battle.

64,000 men strong, take a position in C. The Austrians, to cover their right flank, form a crotchet; their position is shown in A A A.

The Count Schwerin traverses the marshes, and proceeds to D, his left wing formed by his cavalry. The right wing of the Austrians, forming the crotchet, partly changes its front, and takes position in B B, their cavalry being opposite that of the Prussians. By this movement they leave a space of a few hundred yards between their right wing and main body. The king, perceiving this fault, proceeds with a part of his army to occupy this space; the Austrian right wing, attacked on all sides, is completely separated from the center, and obliged to retreat in an eccentric direction from the main army, which is now attacked in its flank and rear by Frederick's whole forces, and driven into Prague, where it is blockaded for several weeks.

This battle, as well as that of Leuthen, shows well that Frederick knew how to fall with his whole force on the weak point of the enemy, and defeat him by a series of small fights. It shows, at the same time, the danger of a crotchet, which, if without any space between it and the main body, is exposed to a very destructive concentric fire.

The Austrians, in this battle, lost 16,000 men and 200 pieces of cannon. The Prussian loss amounted to nearly 13,000 men.

EXAMPLE OF A BATTLE OF THE OFFENSIVE DEFENSE.

BATTLE OF TALAVERA, JULY 28, 1809.

The battle of Talavera, fought by the French against the allied English and Spaniards, offers a very fine example of a defensive battle with offensive return in its own lines. The French army numbered 45,000 men, commanded by King Joseph Bonaparte. The allied army amounted to almost 20,000 English, and 35,000 Spaniards, commanded by Wellington. The Spanish position, forming the right wing of the allies, is covered by two redoubts, and the access to it is rendered so difficult that the French army does not even try an attack, but sends simply a body of dragoons to reconnoiter and observe this spot. The center, composed of four English brigades, is placed between the redoubt on the Spanish left wing and a hill lying in the same front as the two redoubts. The left wing is formed by the regiments defending the hill, by a body of Spanish cavalry under Bassancourt, and by a part of the English cavalry disposed in the valley between the hill and the opposite one. The remainder of the English cavalry, with a part of the Spanish, is formed as reserve behind the hill.

In looking at the line of the English defense, it is easy to see that the hill on the left and the redoubt on the right of the center form like two bastions; that the English center brigades, in retreating only fifty to a hundred yards behind the front line of those two bastions, form the curtain between them; and that, if the enemy advances in the free space left, he is assailed on his right by the fire from the hill, on his

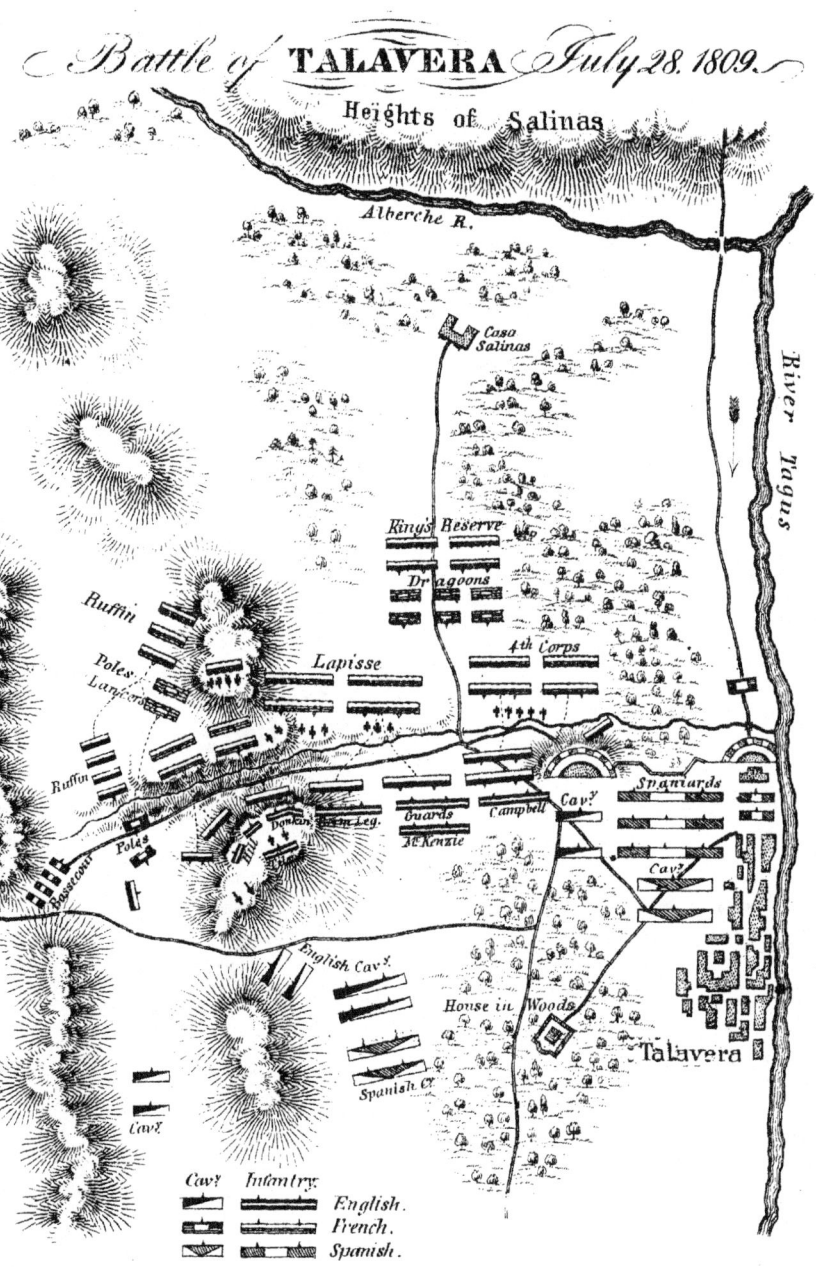

left by that from the redoubt, and in front by that of the brigades; besides, behind the redoubt cavalry is arranged to attack at any moment the flank of an advancing enemy.

The hill forms the key of the position; the French tried in vain to take it; their columns in the valley, in advancing, were exposed to the fire of the English as well as to the charges of their cavalry. In the center the French were more fortunate; the English line, first exposed to a destructive fire, and then attacked by the French columns, gave way, but, as soon as the French advanced, they felt the advantage of the position; attacked in flank by an English regiment descending the hill, exposed on all sides to a deadly fire, and charged by a body of cavalry, their advance was checked, and time was given to the English regiments in the center to form again. The loss on both sides was heavy, and the armies remained in presence of each other the whole night; the next morning the French retreated in complete order.

This example shows well that a defensive battle with offensive return, but with the attack taking place in its own lines, although gained, will defeat a part of the enemy's army, but never, or at least very seldom, his whole force.

EXAMPLE OF A BATTLE OF THE OFFENSIVE DEFENSE.

BATTLE OF AUSTERLITZ, DECEMBER 2, 1805.

Very different from the last battle is that of Austerlitz, which is a defensive battle with offensive return, fought by Napoleon, but offensive in the space in advance of his line of battle. Here the destruction of nearly a whole army was the consequence. This battle took place on the 2d of December, 1805. Napoleon had assembled about 70,000 men near Brünn, and awaited, in a position chosen by himself, the attack of the allied Austrians and Russians, whose army amounted to 84,000 men. His plan was to advance from his own position the moment the enemy attacked him, and to fall on their center with his concentrated forces, while his wings arrested the advance of the enemy's. The first partial victory obtained in the center, the disengaged forces then turn to the right and left, and attack the enemy's wings in their flank.

The allies advance with more than 50,000 men against Napoleon's right wing, composed only of about 5000 men, but afterward reinforced to 12,000 men. The advance of those 50,000 men on the left wing of the allies leaves a free space between their two wings, which is occupied by only a very small force. Napoleon advances there, divides by his movement the allied army in two parts, and defeats each wing separately. The allies lost about 30,000 men, 130 guns, and the remainder of their army was very much scattered.

This battle also serves as an example of an order of battle with reinforced center.

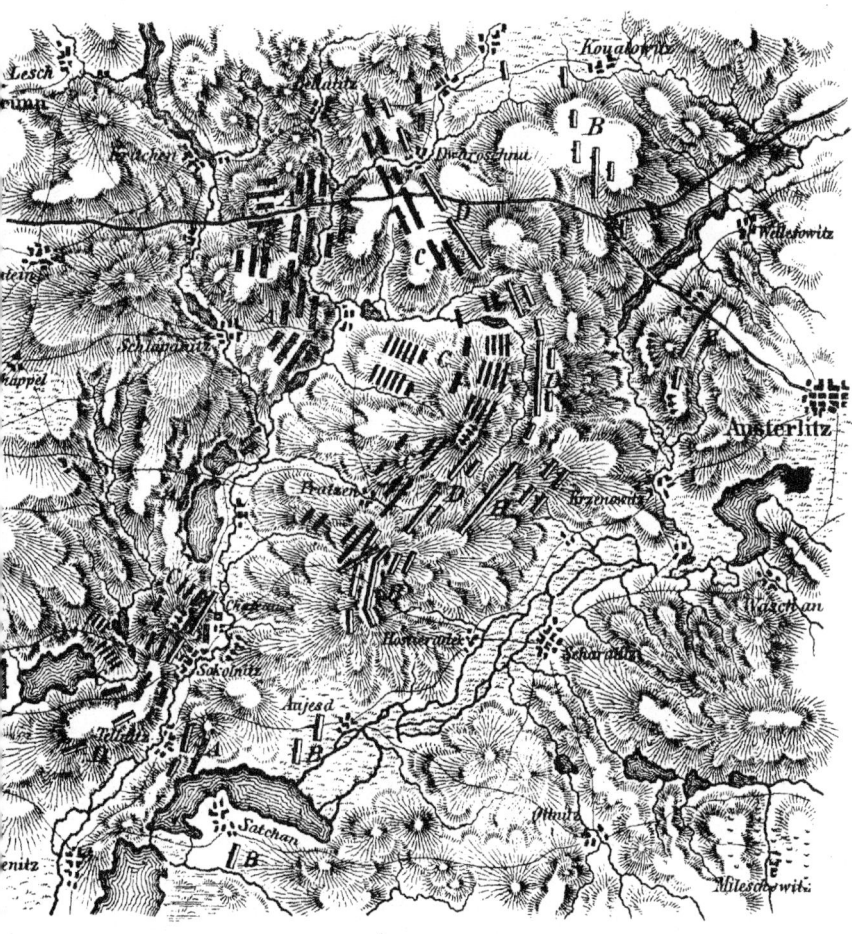

A. First position of the French.
B. First position of the Allies.
C. Position of the French in moment of the Attack.
D. Position of the Allies   „   „   „   „   „   .

USE OF THE THREE ARMS,

COMBINED OR SEPARATE.

In the last chapter, we have seen the general character and disposition of battles, without making any distinction between the three arms. We will now proceed to examine their use, and the rôle they play either separately or combined.

Every battle is composed of a series of fights, which may take place between troops employing but one arm—either of Infantry, Cavalry, or Artillery—or between troops belonging to the three arms united.

If, for instance, we take an army of five brigades engaged in a battle, and forming, we will suppose, an oblique line of battle, each of the brigades will have to keep up a separate fight, in which it may have to act against infantry or cavalry, or against the three arms together.

It is evident that the brigade, being only a part of the whole line of battle, cannot be formed in an oblique order itself; it can only manœuvre, as well as each of the three arms it is composed of, according to the small tactics of its country.

The general principles of formation of troops for fight have already been explained under normal battle arrangements; we must, however, pass in review the chief formations as given in the small tactics, and see in what cases they are to be employed.

INFANTRY.

Infantry can be arranged for fight as follows:—
1. In line.
    a. Open. Skirmishers.
    b. Close. Line of battalion with two or three ranks.
2. In column.
    a. Column of battalion formed from the line on the two center platoons.
    b. Column of companies formed from the line.
3. In squares.
    a. Hollow.
    b. Full.

The open or skirmisher line is extended over a large space; therefore it cannot act with great effect on one special point. All the men in this line act simultaneously; their action is short, and exhaustion soon follows, be it from fatigue or from the using up of the ammunition. The more we increase the number of men in the skirmisher line, the greater will be the loss to the enemy, but also to ourselves, besides the exhaustion of a greater number of our own men. Skirmisher lines are employed to scour the ground in advance of our battalions, to clear it of skirmishers sent out by the enemy, and to keep him at a distance from our lines. We may use a strong or a weak skirmisher line, according to circumstances.

In general, strong skirmisher lines only should be employed where they have to prepare for a decided advance; and where we have special corps to fulfill this task, then entire battalions may be dissolved for skirmishing.

GRAND TACTICS.

If we are obliged to take skirmishers from our line of battle, from the battalions we employ there, we should be careful not to use too many, as all those men we take for skirmishing cannot well be employed at the decisive moment; and we may add that, in skirmishing, we never arrive at a decisive result, and we forget but too easily, in those distant fights, the real object of the engagement.

In close line, the battalion is arranged in two or three ranks, and occupies, if numbering 1000 men, from 200 to 300 yards in length, and $1\frac{1}{2}$ to 2 yards in depth.

The close line acts on a large space; its action is, therefore, not intense on one point, though more so than that of the skirmisher line; all its men act simultaneously. Occupying a large space, and obliged to keep in order, its advance or retreat is rendered difficult in consequence of the configuration of the ground.

The line is, therefore, more adapted for a standing fight, where fire-arms are principally used.

Formed in line, we may await an advancing enemy by firing on him up to the last moment; and then, as soon as his advancing column charges our line, the wings of it take his column in flank, and, by putting at once a greater amount of forces to work, we may oblige him to retreat. Wherever we wish to make use of our fire, we are obliged to adopt the line; besides, the ravages of cannon-shot are not so great in a line as they are in a column, because the shot, in passing through them, will carry away as many men as there are ranks, and the column is always composed of at least four times as many ranks as the line. But if exposed to heavy infantry fire, the line suffers more than the column.

Infantry, if without cover, and exposed to artillery fire from the enemy, is therefore generally disposed in line.

Columns of battalions, Fig. 1, Plate III., formed from the line on the two center platoons. (I suppose the columns formed on the center platoons, because their deploying in line is easier than if formed on the platoons of the wing.) The columns of battalion occupy but 35 to 50 yards front, and about 30 in depth.

In the column we have a successive action; the space is restricted, and the forces are more concentrated on one point. The action of the first rank is followed by that of the second, and so on.

The column can better move than the line; it occupies less space and encounters less difficulties on its march; it is the formation generally used for attack, in which movement is the first necessity. The column cannot fight on its march; it must, therefore, pass as quickly as possible the distance between itself and the enemy, who uses the time of advance to prepare it the greatest possible losses.

The column, in approaching the enemy, acts by impulse; anything that retards the impulse of the column endangers its effect. Very large ones—Fig. 13, Plate III.—as, for instance, used by Napoleon—one division of 12 battalions in column, each battalion deployed and placed one behind the other—were always attended with bad results.

Broken ground, or any other obstacle, rendering the advance of a column slow, will partly destroy its effect.

Columns of company, Fig. 2 and Fig. 3, Plate III., formed from the line, are sometimes used.

The space on which small columns act is restricted; but

the entire space is large, and even larger than that of the line. A battalion formed in such columns encounters as many difficulties in its advance as the line; besides, the command ceases, and this mode of forming tends to too great a division of forces, instead of a concentration.

Those columns, in their advance, can never act simultaneously; some of them always arrive before the others, in consequence of the ground. Those columns should only be employed on well-covered ground, where the acting in mass of the battalion is impossible.

Squares.—Fig. 4 and Fig. 5, Plate III. Intermediary formations between columns and lines. We have hollow squares, approaching more to the line, and full squares, approaching more to the column; the first is a good formation for a battalion remaining stationary, the second for one that is obliged to move. Squares are used against cavalry attacks, being more exposed to such attacks in moving than in remaining stationary; the full square should be more particularly employed than the hollow one, though it presents some disadvantages.

CAVALRY.

Cavalry can only act while moving.

A regiment of cavalry can be arranged in fighting order as follows:—
   1. In line.
     a. Open. Skirmisher line.
     b. Close.

2. In column.
   a. Open, or with distance.
   b. Close.

Open line.—The action of cavalry in open line extended over a large space is like that of infantry fighting in the same order. No intense effort can be made in this order on one point; obstacles of little resistance only can be surmounted.

The loss, in this order, is small.

We use the skirmisher line whenever we are obliged to act against skirmishers of the enemy, against foraging parties, infantry in great disorder, or against artillery of the enemy.

This line has always the disadvantage in acting against close line or columns.

In close line.—Fig. 9, Plate III. Squadrons are arranged one beside the other, but separated by a space of 6 to 12 yards; the squadron itself is arranged in one or two ranks.

The close line is more compact than the open one; it acts, however, on a large space, and demands much room for its formation as well as action. It is generally used by light cavalry. Against an open line, against infantry in disorder or too small squares, and against infantry in march, this formation is the best suited.

Close column.—Fig. 10, Plate III. Squadrons are placed one behind the other, at a distance equal to the front of a platoon augmented by 10 to 15 yards. This order is a compact one, and corresponds with the column of battalion. Its space of action is restricted; it acts by the impulse of the whole mass more than by that of each part

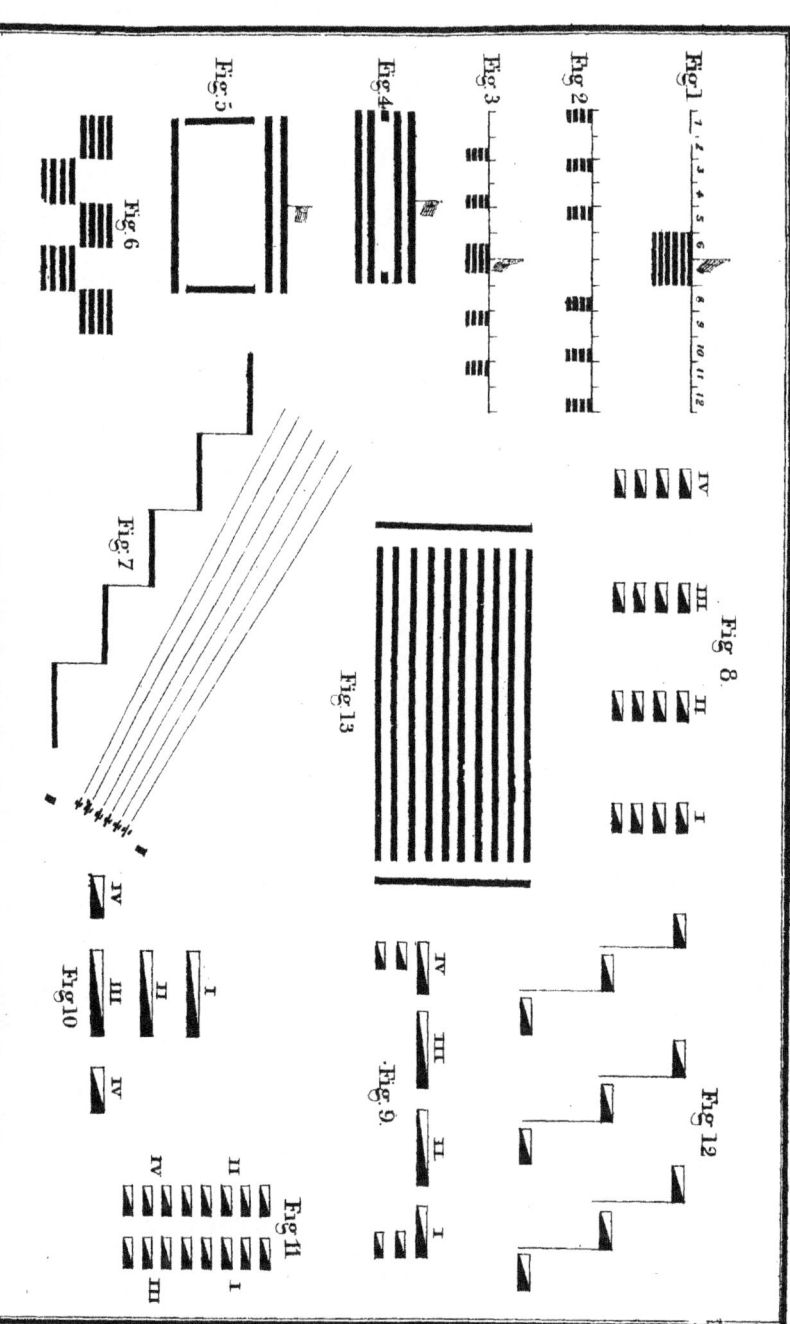

Plate III.

separately. It is of the first importance that all parts forming the front should act simultaneously. Good order is the principal requisition; too quick a gait should not be used; the trot-out is the best suited for this order. It is principally used by heavy cavalry in charging that of the enemy.

If we traverse a space in which we are exposed to losses, we may adopt a quicker gait; but then the squadrons should not follow each other too closely; the rout of the first would involve the others; for such charges we must therefore employ

Open columns.—Fig. 12, Plate III. The squadrons are placed one behind the other, or in echelon, distant from each other one squadron front augmented by about 12 yards.

This order is generally used in charges against infantry, being able to resist and to form into squares.

Cavalry is easily thrown into disorder, and difficult to form again; it must, therefore, be provided with large reserves, and be arranged in deep order. Besides, as in cavalry engagements all actions pass with exceeding rapidity, and as the most exposed part of cavalry while charging is its flank, several platoons are generally disposed on the two wings to cover them, and to take the enemy in flank while charging ours. (See Figs. 9 and 10.)

ARTILLERY.

Artillery acts by batteries.—When stationary and firing, batteries are arranged in line; when moving, they may do so either in line or in column.

While firing, the guns are distant from each other from 25 to 30 or 10 to 12 yards; the latter interval is used when we wish to concentrate the fire.

Batteries have not yet been arranged in columns for firing; this may perhaps be done with rifled guns, which fire at great distances, and with which we may fire over our own troops or artillery in first line.

When fighting, artillery can fire by volleys, or each gun by order, or as soon as it is charged; the second is generally used on the battle-field, the last only in extraordinary cases where delay would be dangerous.

Artillery can act in single batteries or *en masse*.

EACH OF THE THREE ARMS IN THE ATTACK OR DEFENSE.

By what has already been said, it is easy to conclude in what way troops should be disposed for fighting offensively or defensively.

For an offensive battle, in which we are the attacking party, *movement* is the main requisition; therefore the principal mode of formation will be the column. A brigade destined to execute an attack would be disposed as shown in Fig. 6, Plate III. If the space in which the attack takes place is larger than the front of this brigade, another one

GRAND TACTICS.

should be disposed, in a similar way, on its side, by alternate masses of battalions.

Various modes of disposing troops in the attack have been tried—to advance in line deployed; or to advance one battalion in line deployed, and one battalion on each wing in columns; or to advance in large columns, like Fig. 13. All these diverse dispositions are, however, not so practical as that given in Fig. 6, which is now generally employed.

The attack in columns of company is an impossibility as soon as it is executed by more than one or two battalions; and, even then, it should be resorted to only when the ground is too much covered to permit of the action of an entire battalion.

The attack itself should always be preceded by clouds of skirmishers, to protect the front and flank of the advancing columns; to drive back the skirmishers of the enemy; to prevent them from shooting the officers of the advancing troops; and, arriving near the enemy's line, to damage it as much as possible; to direct their fire principally on the officers, and to bring the line in disorder before the shock of the two masses really takes place.

The improvement in fire-arms generally conducts the men and officers to a desire of prolonging the distant fight; *this should be carefully avoided when we act offensively*, as the defending army is mostly favored by the ground it acts on, and naturally wishes a fight, which is never decisive, and in which our loss is probably greater than its own. The relative strength of the combatants remains nearly the same; the decisive moment is retarded or even totally missed, and the loss we sustain in the distant fight is a pure sacrifice of men. It is not a retreat in good order to which we must force our enemy, but one in disorder, in which we can break or cripple a part of his army with little or no loss to ourselves. Such a retreat can only be obtained by the struggle at close quarters.

The principal formation for the defense is the deployed line, which may be also arranged in alternate masses of battalions or in echelons. The last disposition is more solid, especially for a wing which we do not intend to have reinforced, or for which we have only few troops to spare. Fig. 7, Plate III., shows a similar disposition. An advancing enemy is always taken in flank, either by the battery on the extreme wing or by the regiments above or below the one attacked. The distance between two battalions is generally equal to the front of one of them deployed in line.

There is one great maxim for every defense, whatever be our disposition, whether in echelons or alternate masses, which is—*After having delivered a well-directed volley at short distance, to encounter an advancing enemy by our own advance.*

By acting on this principle, the English lines nearly always defeated the French columns, during the Peninsular war. The English battalions, disposed in deployed lines of two ranks, were posted thirty to forty yards behind the ridge of steep hills; the columns, arriving breathless on this spot, received first a volley at half pistol-shot distance, which laid low nearly the whole of the first rank, and were then assailed with the bayonet, and invariably thrown down the hill.

When our line of battle is composed of alternate masses

of battalions, and if the first line is strongly pressed and obliged to retreat, the second line, which is always disposed in columns, should advance, and pass the intervals in advancing, and not wait till they are passed by the first line in retreating. This is necessary, as well for the order as for the *morale* of the troops; and, besides, it has the advantage of permitting our disordered battalions sooner to form again, before the disorder has become too great, and of better checking the advance of the enemy.

If infantry is obliged to act against cavalry alone, it forms in order of battle; but, instead of disposing in line or column, the battalions are disposed in squares. These can also be formed by an entire brigade. The batteries are generally disposed on the corners of the squares, being their weakest points.

When cavalry is the fighting troop, we may arrange it in various ways. It can never act defensively; and even if inferior, and attacked, it must defend itself by attacking.

Being easily brought into disorder, it must be arranged in deep order of battle; when several regiments are united, and have to form in line of battle, the first line may be arranged by squadrons deployed in line, as the ravages of artillery are less; the intervals between two regiments are equal to the front of one squadron. In the intervals, but four or five hundred yards behind, is arranged the second line, either in close column or in columns of squadrons by platoons. Fig. 11, Plate III. Besides this second line, the reserve is kept in readiness a few hundred yards behind it. There exist many other battle arrangements for cavalry; there are now, however, few civilized countries in which large masses of cavalry can act.

In all cavalry engagements, the party who keeps the best order during the charge will, everything else being equal, be successful; after a charge, the victorious cavalry is in just as much confusion as the defeated; and if, at this moment, it is charged itself, defeat will be sure to follow; besides, charges on the flank of charging cavalry are nearly always attended with success; from this it results that, in cavalry engagements, a rapid *coup d'œil*, by the commanding officer, is of the greatest importance—sparing his forces, so as to have the last reserve to give out, and always engaging at the right moment his different squadrons, will assuredly give him the advantage over even a stronger enemy.

In acting against infantry formed in squares, it would seem that quickly succeeding charges, but executed each time only with a limited number of men, are more advantageous than those executed by too large a mass. The squadrons are then generally disposed in open column or in echelons. Fig. 12, Plate III. The first squadron arriving near the infantry deprives it of its fire for the succeeding squadrons; and it is difficult, with the bayonet alone, to prevent cavalry breaking the ranks of infantry.

However, it must be stated that cavalry should generally only charge infantry in disorder or while marching, as in acting against infantry which is *not* so, and which has time to form in squares, its loss is heavy and unnecessary.

Artillery never acts alone; it is always accompanied by one of the two other arms.

GRAND TACTICS.

Smooth-bored guns open fire at about 1600 to 1700 yards; at these distances shots are fired: from 1100 to 1400 yards, and, if the ground permits it, they are fired by ricochet, or rolled; from 600 to 1200 yards, spherical case or shrapnels; and under 600 yards, canister is fired.

Against deployed lines, shrapnel and canister, and against columns, shrapnel and shot are the most advantageous.

Rifled guns commence firing sooner; the projectiles used are shells; shrapnels, and canister, the last only at short distances.

When acting against artillery of the enemy, our batteries should be disposed so as to take his batteries *en echarpe*, or to place them in a concentric fire.

In forming large batteries of 40, 50, or even 100 guns, they can be disposed in one continued battery, or in small ones having sufficient intervals to permit the passage of the advancing battalions; both methods may be employed according to circumstances.

In artillery engagements more than in any others, it is of the utmost importance not to disperse our spare or reserve batteries, but always to concentrate an overwhelming fire on one point.

THE THREE ARMS COMBINED.

In fight two kinds of arms are used, fire-arms and steel, (*l'arme blanche.*) One represents the distant fight, and the other that at close quarters.

In consequence of the action of those two kinds of arms, we distinguish four different periods; of these each fight is composed.

1st. Introduction.
2d. Advance and preparation.
3d. Close quarters.
4th. Retreat or pursuit.

The two first periods belong to the fire-arms, the two last to the steel.

Infantry is provided with arms for both fights.

Artillery is used only for distant fight, cavalry for that at close quarters.

Infantry acts in all of the four periods; artillery, principally in the two first; and cavalry, in the two last.

Artillery prepares, cavalry completes, the work of infantry.

Infantry forms the really acting body of our whole line of battle; artillery assists it in the beginning, cavalry at the end, of its action.

Although the armament indicates so clearly the use of the three arms, we see, nearly every day, the greatest mistakes made in their employment. In these cases it is generally cavalry that is the sufferer; but infantry likewise is sometimes the victim, if the artillery has not been made a right use of in the beginning of the action.

To show well the succeeding and simultaneous action of the three arms, let us suppose A B the enemy's line of battle, Plate IV., and our army consisting of five brigades, two of which we have in reserve and three in line of battle, as shown in the normal battle arrangements.

Introduction.

Each fight, when not intended to surprise the enemy, has an introduction.

In placing our army in the position M N, we cannot march at once to M' N'; we do not know exactly the enemy's position, neither do we know the strength of his forces; we must first see if it be prudent to engage in a fight, and if we may be aggressive, or if, by the superiority of the enemy, we would become defensive.

From the columns of march we must arrange our army in line of battle; we must reconnoiter the ground, and find out the best points of attack; all this takes a certain time, and is therefore called the Introduction.

Our army arrived at long cannon ranges, we put some of our batteries in position, and open a slow and measured fire; we send our skirmishers in advance to scour and clear the ground we wish to occupy; we send also some detachments of cavalry as far as the enemy's first line of battle, to reconnoiter his position and strength.

The enemy will probably answer our first proceedings in a similar way; in the mean time our army draws near, and arrives at really effective cannon ranges, and the first period gradually passes to the second.

Advance and Preparation.

In consequence of the counter disposition of the enemy, as well as the information received from our reconnoitering parties, we have been able to form an idea of his arrangements and his strength; we have seen and reflected; we must now begin to act.

We have chosen our points of attack; and it is there we must proceed against the enemy, and drive him from his position.

The advance of our troops, however, must be prepared; our batteries must be put in position, with orders to keep up a continuous fire; our skirmishers must advance by degrees, and we must drive the enemy from any post he has taken in advance of his whole line of battle.

Artillery plays the principal rôle in this period of the fight. The few batteries we have already placed in line should multiply themselves by their great energy and by their quick and rapid manœuvres. They should act by whole batteries, and not by sections. Their duty is to find out the points where they can do the enemy the greatest damage, drawing near his battalions, delivering a short and well-directed fire, changing their position to act against another battalion, appearing where the enemy least expects them, where his battalions, behind cover, thought themselves well screened, disappearing before the enemy can make any attempt to drive them away, reappearing to spread disorder and loss in another direction, directing an overwhelming fire of shells and shrapnels against the astonished enemy, and spreading fear and terror through his whole line of battle,—this is the way artillery should act. Only light rifled guns, as now employed in Europe, can accomplish such work.

In this period, artillery has principally to fire against

the enemy's cavalry and infantry; if, however, two of our batteries can unite their efforts, they may by their superiority silence one of the enemy's batteries. To do this, they should advance in echelons by sections; some of the guns should fire shrapnels, to prevent a quick serving of the enemy's battery, and the others should try to dismount some of his guns by continually directing their united efforts on one gun; if they succeed in dismounting this, they should then proceed to another. They should, in this operation, take such positions that their fire is concentric; at the same time that one battery fires at the enemy in front the other should rake him.

While this action of artillery is taking place, we should make our arrangements for the principal attack; the enemy, on account of our decided action, has put more forces in position, and we have had ample time to choose the point where we intend to break his line.

The armies having gradually drawn nearer, in some parts our first line is already engaged in a distant fight with the enemy's, and everything predicts the quick approach of the third period. But we must render our success certain. C D, in the figure, is the point where we must gain our first partial victory. Opposite C D we place our artillery of reserve, forming one large battery of 60 to 70 guns, arranged in batteries, with small intervals, and concentrating their fire on C D. In this part we dissolve entire battalions into skirmisher lines, to clear and prepare the advance for our batteries and battalions; we bring our reserve nearer; we arrange our infantry in columns of attack; we place our cavalry in readiness on the flanks and in the rear of our great mass, and then we order the advance.

Our skirmishers repulse quickly those of the enemy by their great superiority in number. Our reserve batteries open fire, advancing in echelons by batteries. They silence first those of the enemy; this accomplished, they concentrate their fire on his battalions. Our infantry follows the movements of the artillery, and advances; arrived at canister ranges, the artillery delivers its last rounds, and our battalions pass the open space and fall on the weakened enemy.

The artillery should continue its fire till that of each gun is masked by the advancing columns; then, if our batteries are composed of rifled guns, they should at once commence to damage the enemy's reserve by firing shells over our own troops in the direction in which this reserve is probably placed.

Close Quarters.

This is certainly the most critical moment of the battle. Our columns, in approaching the enemy's battalions, may deploy in line, and, by a very vigorous fire, drive them from their position, or they may continue their march in column, and attack them with the bayonet. The last is preferable, as the column, being once stopped and deployed, cannot be easily formed again; besides, the men, once in motion, and excited by the whole scene around them, are much more fit for dealing blows than for cool shooting; and finally, besides all this, the enemy might just choose the moment we are deploying to fall himself on us. If our advance is well prepared, if our skirmishers, placed in the intervals of the advancing columns, keep up to the last moment a well-sustained fire, if our troops advance firmly toward the enemy, if the head of the columns, arrived at ten or twelve yards from his line, delivers its fire and then falls on the enemy with a shout, there are no soldiers in the whole world that could resist such an attack. Wherever they have resisted, the two first periods have been badly conducted. Real bayonet encounters in open field seldom or never take place, as one of the two parties generally turns back and retreats.

But the difficulty is much less to take than to keep the enemy's position. Our columns, in falling on the enemy, become disbanded and disordered; at this moment the enemy advances with his second line sustained by his reserves. In advancing in the enemy's position, we expose our flanks, and we are deprived of our artillery and cavalry; the enemy, on the other hand, has assembled those three arms for our reception; his artillery plays on us, raking us; its action is followed by charges of cavalry on our flank, and at the same time we are attacked in front by fresh regiments just arrived. Thousands of examples show that, if our already victorious first line is well received, it must yield. The Crimean war and the last Italian war offer many such examples.

Our first line is driven back and retreats behind our second, which advances to sustain it; our cavalry charges the advancing cavalry of the enemy or his pursuing regiments; such of our guns as can be brought to bear reopen their fire. Our columns reassemble again, and form behind the artillery, which recommences to batter the position of the enemy; fresh troops advance for the struggle, till, finally, we gain the position, and force the enemy to retreat, or till we ourselves are obliged to do so. The one who has most spared his forces, and who has best understood how to make them act at the right moment, will obtain the victory. At the battle of Solferino, the Austrian center was attacked three times, and succumbed only at the third advance; it was deprived, in this critical moment, of its cavalry, which might, if it had been present, have turned the victory of the disbanded French columns into a retreat.

Retreat or Pursuit.

If the second period of the distant fight belongs principally to artillery, the second period of the close-quarter fight belongs chiefly to cavalry. Cavalry should fall on the retreating and shaken battalions of the enemy to disperse and destroy them. When they are in disorder, the charge should take place at once, so as to leave them no time to form again; where they are still in order, a few guns, with which cavalry should always be provided, should advance to very effective canister ranges, deliver a few well-directed rounds, which should be immediately followed by an impetuous charge. Cavalry should thus convert into a *rout* the *retreat* to which the enemy has been forced by the infantry.

Wherever the enemy wishes to stop to rally his forces, he should be attacked immediately and with great energy; to

GRAND TACTICS. 129

accomplish this fully, our cavalry should be always well supported by infantry and artillery. The final pursuit of an entirely disordered and disbanded enemy generally belongs to cavalry alone.

The defense in those four periods should be similar to the attack, only that it should be more careful of its forces, and not give out its artillery too quickly; its principal moment for action should be from the time the fire of the attacking party has ceased and the enemy's columns are advancing to close. This is the moment for the defense to bring a part of its reserve artillery in position, to fire canister on the advancing columns; its battalions, reinforced by reserves, deploy in line, and open a well-sustained fire; and finally, if the columns arrive at 15 to 20 yards, those lines deliver their last round, and, falling on the astonished and weakened columns, drive them back; its cavalry, kept in readiness, will charge at the same moment the attacking battalions in flank, and pursue them as far as their own lines. The cavalry of the defense can charge against the enemy when he traverses the free space; this is always dangerous; if the attacking battalions are not already weakened, the charge takes place better in the moment following the attack of the two lines, whatever be the result of this attack, because the victorious, as well as the defeated, will be in disorder. If forced to retreat, the defense should arrange those of the reserves, or those regiments which have suffered the least, in line of battle behind the spot where the main attack took place, to cover the retreat of the defeated troops; it should try to rally those troops, and make the best use of its artillery, and principally of its cavalry; the loss of a few guns should not be considered, if time is gained to form again the troops and to obtain an advance on the pursuing enemy.

Conclusion.

The fight, as described, generally takes place when well-disciplined troops are opposed. It is not necessary to say that our whole disposition, and the time of the four different periods, should differ according to the importance of the attack or to the character of the enemy. To deal with Mexican or Neapolitan soldiers, we need not pay much attention as regards introduction and preparation; the more boldly we act the greater will be the success. I was told by an eye-witness of the battle of the Volturno, in 1860, that a band of English sailors belonging to a British man-of-war, having leave to go ashore, were present to see the fight. Carried away by the excitement of the whole scene around them, they advanced and found themselves at once in the vicinity of a Neapolitan battery, just commencing its fire. With one impulse the unarmed English tars rushed to the battery, stormed it, and drove away the cannoneers; at the same moment the battalion for the cover of the battery advanced to attack them with the bayonet, but the battalion shared the same fate as the cannoneers— they were literally boxed out of the battery, which then turned its fire on its proper owners. Any ammunition spent against such soldiers would evidently be a loss; the bayonet and sword are quite sufficient to settle every difficulty. Besides the character, the strength of the enemy opposed to us, as well as the importance of the point of attack, will

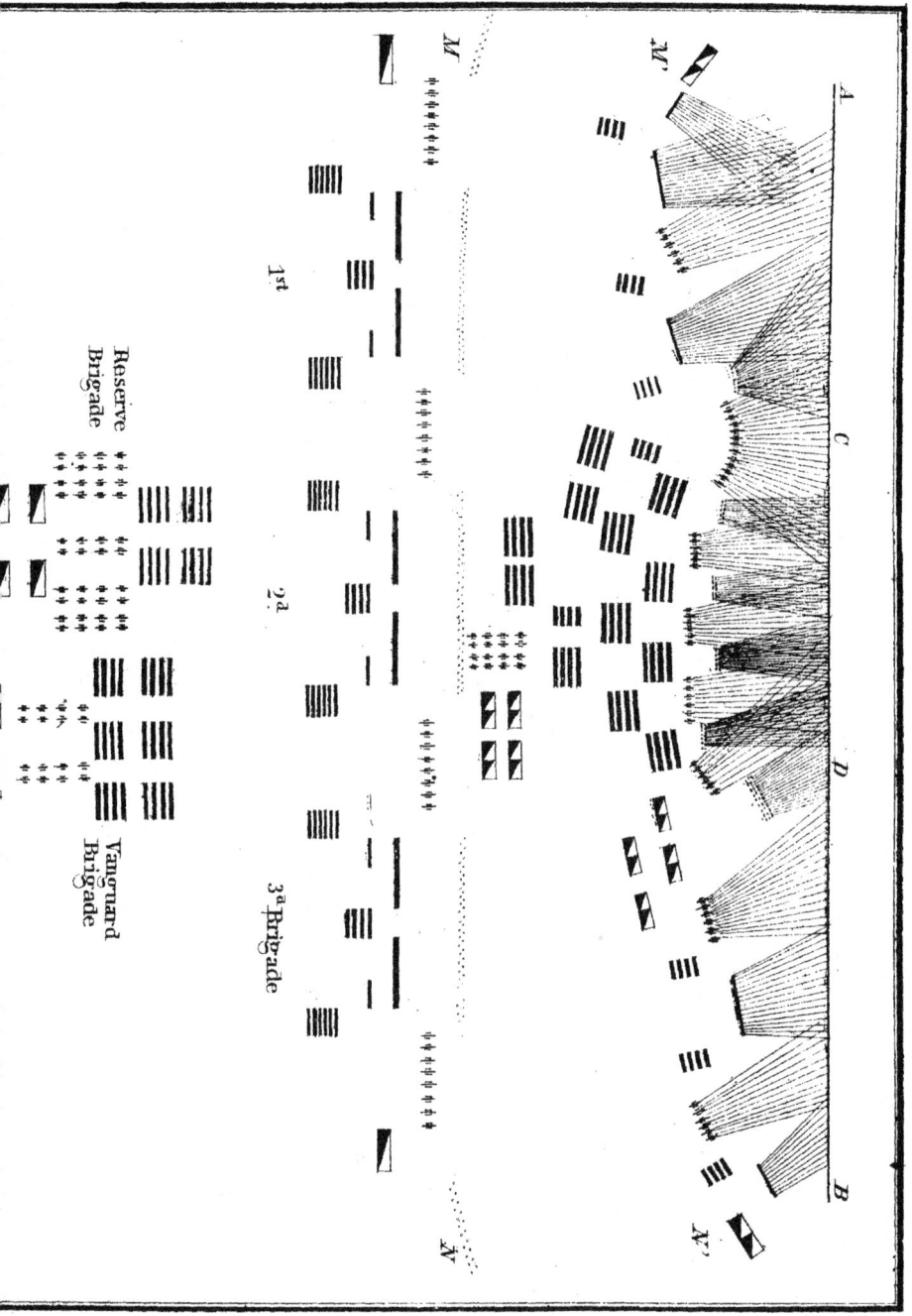

much change the length of the periods. Secondary points are attacked with less means, and defended with less. We have no reserve artillery on these places. Our batteries of brigade must do their best. Infantry will act more in distant fight. Neither of the two parties will risk a decisive blow without being sure of success; the closing takes place after a greater length of time, when one of the parties has gained, in the second period, an ascendant over the other. If we are very superior to the enemy, our action should be short and decisive. We should make the distant fight as short but as powerful as possible, and advance with our masses to crush him.

We conclude, from all that has been said—

1st. That we should concentrate our principal forces, and keep them in reserve to strike the decisive blow on the most important point at the right moment.

2d. That on all other parts of the battle-field we should place only the necessary amount of forces to keep back the enemy for the length of time required.

3d. That we should act with superior forces on a restricted part of the battle-field.

4th. That we should make a right use of the three arms in the four different periods.

5th. That great artillery attacks, executed with a number of batteries, should first silence the fire of the enemy's artillery before commencing to batter his troops.

6th. That the fire of artillery at short ranges should continue till the weakened state of the enemy becomes manifest.

7th. That strong and reinforced skirmisher lines should

be employed only to precede a decisive attack, or to resist such an attack of the enemy.

8th. That our advance, to close with the enemy, should take place in columns, proceeding at the quickest pace, but only after the enemy is already in such a state that the losses he can prepare for our columns will not give him the superiority in the moment of the shock.

9th. That in the defense, after having kept up a destructive fire, we should, in the last moment, pass to the offensive, and attack the enemy ourselves.

10th. That cavalry should act only against infantry which is unable at the moment to make a regular use of its firearms—meaning that cavalry should avoid all engagements where it is exposed to a well-ordered distant fight.

11th. Finally, that in every fight we should consider the object we wish to attain, our means and those of the enemy, and, principally, the character of the troops opposed to us.

It is necessary to say a few words on turning an enemy's army or his flank on the field of battle, and also on the attack of intrenched camps.

At all times, and with many generals, the idea of turning an enemy was a favorite one; and history offers just as many examples where these attacks have been successful as where they have not been so.

As a general rule, it may be observed—

1st. That turning manœuvres should only be executed when we have a decided superiority over the enemy.

2d. That no large circuitous movements should be made, for, while they are being executed, the main army might be defeated—in other words, our army and the turning corps must remain connected.

3d. When opposed to a distinguished general, the turning of his flank is always dangerous, as in the operation we offer our own flanks to his attack.

4th. An attack in front of a wing in which it is at the same time outflanked, and obliged to form a crotchet, is, at all events, a safer mode than the turning by a separate corps. The battles of the Alma and Wagram may serve as examples.

To show the danger of surrounding, we have but to remember the results of the battles of Austerlitz and Rivoli, gained by Napoleon; that of Stockach, by the Archduke Charles; and that of Salamanca, gained by Wellington.

The plan of the battle of Austerlitz shows the manœuvre of the allies. With their right wing they intended to attack Napoleon in front; with their left, amounting to 50,000 men, they intended to turn him. Napoleon seized the moment when their left wing had advanced to the attack to fall with his main force in the free space left between the right and left wings, which were defeated separately.

At the battle of Rivoli, the Austrian general, Alvinzi, had formed four columns, which were to surround and attack on all sides the small army of Napoleon disposed on the plateau of Rivoli. Napoleon left two of those columns no time to form; he defeated them before they could deploy in order of battle; the main column of Alvinzi was defeated in its turn by Napoleon's entire force; and the fourth column, which had arrived in his rear, was arrested for some time by a few battalions, and, after the defeat of the main body, obliged to surrender.

At Stockach, Jordan, commanding the French army, imitated Alvinzi at Rivoli, and attacked the Archduke Charles in a similar way; Jordan was entirely defeated.

In the attack of intrenched camps, or of field-works in general, we cannot proceed as we do against an army in open field; the enemy is more protected from our fire by the epaulement; and our advance, or rather our closing with him, is rendered difficult by the ditch; besides, in the advance, we are too much exposed to his fire, without being able to return it. On the other hand, the defender of an intrenched camp or redoubt cannot deploy great forces, and cannot himself pass to the offensive at the right moment.

These different circumstances should tell us how to conduct the attack. A converging and overwhelming fire of shells should be directed on one point—if possible, against a corner of the intrenchment—to dismount the artillery of defense, to bring the troops in disorder, and to hinder the disposal of a strong reserve. Heavy masses of skirmishers should advance also in a converging manner against that same point; and small columns of assault should be kept in readiness, but sheltered as much as possible up to the last moment. If the ditch is deep—a serious obstacle to the passage of the troops—every skirmisher, before commencing to fight, should be provided with a fagot, to roll before him, and to serve him, at the same time, as cover. Arrived at the ditch, this should be filled up with those fagots, and the columns which are kept ready should pass immediately to the assault. If the epaulement is steep, the storming column should be provided with ladders. If the redoubts are open behind, cavalry should charge and enter them by the gorge, while the infantry attacks in front, and by this facilitate the action of the storming columns.

In general, it may be said that troops and their commanders who seek safety in intrenched positions, instead of giving open battle, are already half defeated, as they evidently give up all idea of offensive movements, and must quietly await the counter dispositions of the attacking and stronger enemy.

EXAMPLE.

BATTLE OF WATERLOO.

FEW battles have been more often described than the battle of Waterloo; but, having been fought by three different armies, the accounts concerning it are somewhat partial, agreeing with the prejudices of the Englishman, Frenchman, or Prussian who describes it. However, the French and Prussian accounts are more in accordance with each other than either of the two with the English. The following description is taken from French and Prussian authentic reports.

Napoleon, after his return from the Isle of Elba, hoped to open successfully the campaign against the allies by falling on Blücher and Wellington, who, with their armies, amounting to 220,000 men, had taken up their quarters in Belgium. It was Napoleon's intention to act speedily, and thereby surprise and defeat them separately. With astonishing rapidity he concentrated his forces near Charleroi, and, on the 16th of June, found himself and army in the quarters of Blücher, who, however, had managed to assemble the greater part of his forces, about 80,000 men, near Fleurus and Ligny—leaving, in this position, his base of operation on the Rhine, to form a junction with Wellington, who was assembling his troops, that very day, near Quatre-Bras, distant about seven miles from Fleurus.

Napoleon had sent Marshal Ney, with about 40,000 combatants, to attack the forces already at Quatre-Bras, while he himself, with the main body, 65,000 men, attacked the army of Blücher.

Ney, having advanced very late, found the forces at Quatre-Bras too strong, and was obliged to retreat. In the mean time, Napoleon had defeated the Prussians, and forced them to leave the battle-field.

Double mistakes were made this day. Ney, at Quatre-Bras, was already in the rear of Blücher; Napoleon ordered him to leave this position, and to advance to Bry, in order to cut the Prussians from their lines of communication; this order was not received by Ney, but by the general commanding the greater part of his troops, and on his way to support him at Quatre-Bras; he took, in consequence of the new order, the road to Bry, but lost his way, and was called back again by Ney.

Those divisions, composing the 6th army corps, had passed the whole day in marching, and were therefore of no use either in the battle of Ligny or in that of Quatre-Bras.

Napoleon, thinking the Prussians had retreated to Namur, left Grouchy, with 35,000 men, to pursue them, while he advanced to Quatre-Bras, where he joined Ney, and where he anticipated finding Wellington. Wellington had, however, already retreated to Mont St. Jean, and taken a position there, where he was followed by Napoleon, on the 17th of June. It was too late, on this day, to make an attack, the army being very much exhausted; it was, therefore, postponed to the next day, the 18th.

In the mean while, Blücher retreated in the direction of Wavre, where he arrived on the 17th; the corps of Bülow, amounting to 30,000 men, was already there. This corps had taken no part in the battle of Ligny; and, besides, from the 80,000 men present at the battle of the 16th, Blücher could assemble on the 17th about 40,000 or 45,000.

Grouchy had pursued the Prussian army on the 17th, but only as far as Gembloux, where a Prussian rear guard induced him to believe that the whole army was still there.

Wavre is about five or six miles from Mont St. Jean. Blücher and Wellington concerted the measures to be taken for the 18th : Wellington was to keep his position to the last, and Blücher was to arrive and join him in the course of the battle.

Before proceeding further, we must say a few words concerning the strength of the armies, and the configuration of the ground on which the battle took place.

STRENGTH OF THE ARMIES.

Army of Wellington.

	Battal's.	Squad's.	Batt's.	Men.
Anglo-Hanoverians	74	81	21	61,325
Netherlands	38	28	8	28,865
Brunswick	8	5	2	6,658
Nassau	3			2,900
	123	114	31	99,748

From these troops, Wellington detached about 19,000 men to Halle, to cover his right flank on the road from Halle to Brussels. Some smaller detachments, besides the

Movements of the 3 armies preceding the battle of Waterloo

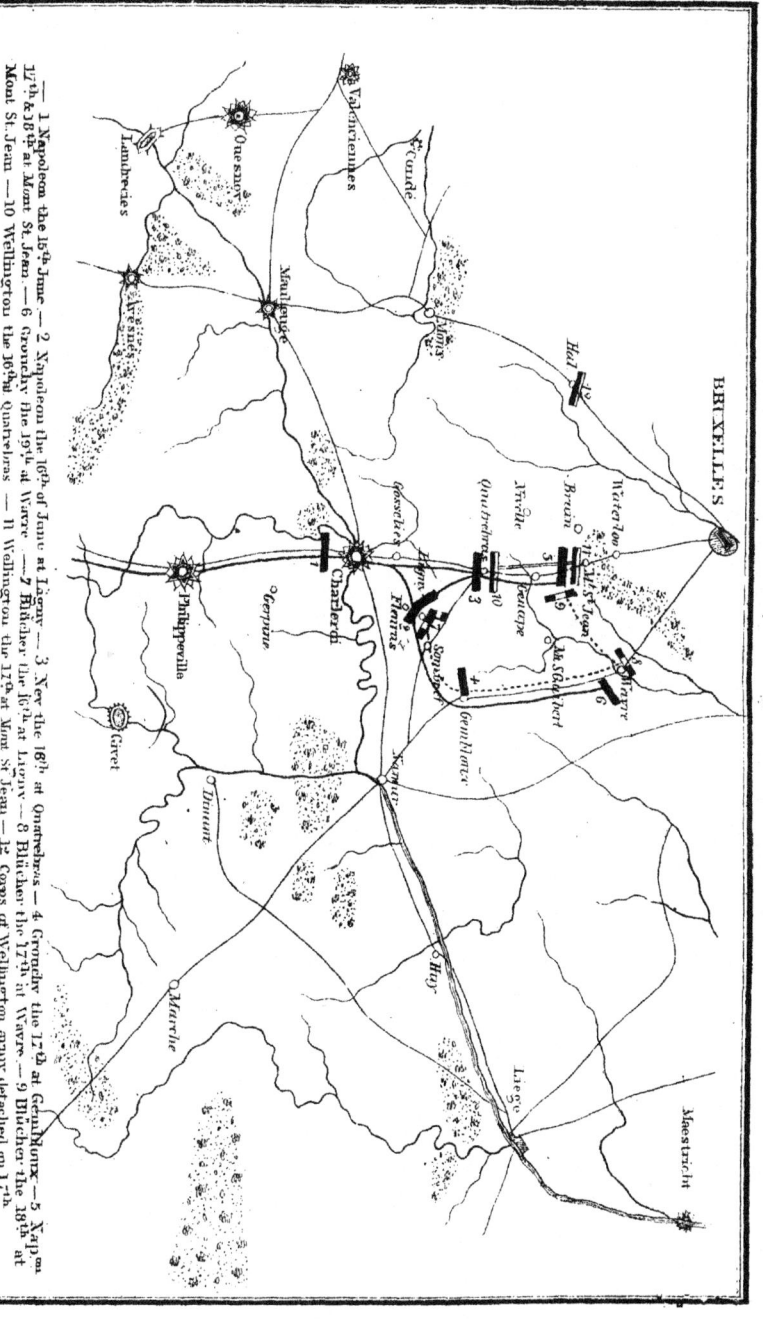

— 1 Napoleon the 15th June — 2 Napoleon the 16th of June at Ligny — 3 Ney the 16th at Quatrebras — 4 Grouchy the 17th at Gembloux — 5 Nap⁰ⁿ 17th & 18th at Mont St Jean — 6 Grouchy the 19th at Wavre — 7 Blücher the 16th at Ligny — 8 Blücher the 17th at Wavre — 9 Blücher the 18th at Mont St Jean — 10 Wellington the 16th at Quatrebras — 11 Wellington the 17th at Mont St Jean — 12 Corps of Wellington army detached on L7th

GRAND TACTICS.   139

loss sustained at Quatre-Bras, reduced the army present at the battle to about 70,000 men.

Army of Napoleon.

	Battal's.	Squad's.	Guns.	Men.
Guard	24	32	96	18,400
Army corps:—				
1st. Count Erlon	32	21	46	20,564
2d. Count Reille	40	15	46	23,926
6th. Count Lobau	18		32	10,932
Cavalry		87	48	10,000
	114	155	268	83,822

Of these 83,822 men, only about 68,000 to 70,000 were present at the battle of Waterloo; the remainder represents the loss in the battles of Ligny and Quatre-Bras, besides the division of Girard, which was with the army of Marshal Grouchy. Several battalions, which had experienced heavy losses on the 16th, were consolidated; the number of battalions present was, therefore, only 97.

The Prussian army, under the command of Marshal Blücher, assembled at Wavre on the morning of the 18th, consisting of—

Four Army Corps:—

	Battal's.	Squad's.	Batt's.	Men.
1st. Gen. Ziethen	34	32	12	30,381
2d. Gen. Pirsch	36	36	10	31,758
3d. Gen. Thielman	30	34	6	23,980
4th. Gen. Bülow	36	43	11	30,328
	136	145	39	116,447

Of these four army corps, that of Bülow was the only one

that took no part in the battle of Ligny on the 16th; the other corps had experienced heavy losses, and the amount of forces disposable was 70,000 to 80,000 men. They were pursued by Marshal Grouchy, with the 3d and 4th French army corps, numbering about 35,000 men.

Battle-field.

The battle-field chosen by the Duke of Wellington lies in advance of Mont St. Jean. The main road from Charleroi to Brussels passes through its center; it forms a kind of upland, gradually sloping on each side of the main road, across which, beyond Mont St. Jean, lies a chain of hills. It was on the top of these hills that the English army was placed; the second line was partly behind them, and sheltered from the French artillery. Belle Alliance and Mont St. Jean are separated by a valley covered by fields. In advance of the English right wing is the Castle of Hougomont, surrounded by a ditch, a large park, and a small wood; the castle was prepared for defense. In the center, near the road, stood a farm, called La Haye Sainte, and likewise prepared for defense. On the left wing were three other farms—Haye, Papelotte, and Smouhen. The village of Planchenois is about half a mile distant from the main road. During the whole night of the 17th it rained in torrents, leaving the fields in a very swampy condition for the morning of the 18th.

Arrangements for Battle.

Wellington's army occupied the heights near Mont St. Jean; two-thirds of his forces composed his right, and one-third his left wing; he hoped that this last one would be soon reinforced by the Prussians. His troops were arranged in lines of two ranks; their principal tactic was the defense, and to act with powerful fire. This is the system the English principally employed in Spain, and which they followed also at Waterloo. Little mobility could be found in their infantry; but their cavalry was very enterprising. The half of Wellington's army was composed of soldiers who had seen service in the preceding campaigns. The French acted principally in columns; they were arranged as shown in the plan.

The object of Napoleon, in this battle, was to destroy the English army; this could only be accomplished by separating it entirely from the Prussian army, and by cutting off its line of retreat to Brussels. There were two ways leading to this result—a main attack on the left wing, or one on the center, of the English position, to gain the road to the Forest of Soignes.

Napoleon planned two attacks—one, a feint attack on the right wing of the English, which was to induce them to reinforce it; and a main attack on the left wing.

The division of Jerome, conducted by Guilleminot, attacks, at nearly twelve o'clock, the wood of Hougomont, and takes possession, after a severe struggle. A brigade of English Guards, conducted by Cook, comes to the rescue of the battalions who defend it, and drive back the French; the troops of Brunswick replace this brigade in their position.

The division of Foy backs the troops of Guilleminot, who is dangerously wounded in the shoulder; he, nevertheless, leads on his troops to the fight, and the park is taken; the wood is disputed, and at last remains in possession of the French.

The division of Bachelu advances between the wood and the main road leading to Charleroi, but is stopped by the Hanoverians and the English brigade of Hackett. In the mean time, Ney has arranged the right wing of the French; eighty guns are in position to batter the left wing of the English; four columns are formed for the attack—one on the left of the farm of La Haye Sainte; one on the center of the left wing, between Papelotte and the main road; the third column is kept as reserve for the two first; and the fourth advances against Papelotte. All these columns have for reserve the cavalry of General Guyot.

During this time, Napoleon has kept back his 6th army corps, his corps of Guards, and his cavalry of reserve, to bring them into action at the decisive moment. The first column advances against La Haye Sainte, and takes it. The second column advances through a heavy fire of artillery from the English position, traverses the space between the two armies, and ascends the hill, where the 95th Regiment is placed. Here the French column is received by a heavy fire from this regiment and the German legion; it turns to the right, and closes with the division of Perponcher.*

---

* OBSERVATION. — The artillery placed in front of the English position to batter the English line was very distant—not nearer than

The English line is broken, and the column advances. The 32d English Regiment meets it, and is furiously attacked; it begins to give way, when the French column is taken in flank by the 42d and 92d Regiments.

The division of Perponcher rallies, in the mean time. The French, attacked on all sides, keep their ground, till they are charged by the second brigade of English cavalry; this cavalry fell afterward on the French reserves and on three batteries, which were just passing through the valley between the two armies to approach more nearly the English line; the horses and men were killed.

Napoleon, seeing this, ordered the cavalry of Milhaud to advance against the English, which, attacked by the Cuirassiers of Milhaud and the French Lancers at the same time, was nearly destroyed.

The second and third columns, after having been repulsed, reassembled in the valley. The French cavalry, after its success against the English cavalry, advanced against La Haye Sainte, to the spot where the action of the first column took place, which had in the mean time been driven back, and pursued by a battalion of Hanoverians; this was

---

1200 yards. The columns of infantry were columns of division, (Fig. 13, Plate III.,) and too large to permit of any free and quick movement; besides, the ground was in such a state that the advance of the columns was very slow. Those large columns require too many men, the greater part of whom is of no use; and, if the heads of the columns are endangered, they have no reserve to support them in time. These facts, as well as that nearly every attack on this day was isolated, are the principal reasons of the failure of this great battle.

charged by the French Cuirassiers, and entirely dispersed. The French cavalry then advanced against the English line, but was charged by the cavalry of Somerset; this was in its turn driven back by that of General d'Homond coming to the assistance of the Cuirassiers of Milhaud.

The French column, being rid of the pursuing Hanoverians, forms again and advances; other Hanoverian battalions advance to the encounter of this French division; they are charged, on their way, by Milhaud's cavalry: two battalions are cut to pieces. Milhaud's men are again forced to retreat by those of Somerset and Dornbery. In the mean time, about one o'clock, Napoleon receives the news of the arrival of Prussian troops near Frischermont, and dispatches General d'Homond, with 3000 horse, to his right wing, where they form a crotchet. Those 3000 horse had supported Marshal Ney in his attack.

On the English right wing nothing of importance had been done; the wood was in the possession of the French, the castle and garden in that of the English. The French had raised batteries against the castle, which began to burn.

Ney, after the repulse of his first attack—which, however, was too isolated, and not properly supported by reserves—had reopened the fire of his batteries, and was again forming his troops.

Preceded by multitudes of skirmishers, the French columns advance to the right and left of the main road; La Haye Sainte, Papelotte, and Smouhen are carried by the French. Napoleon has just disposed the 6th army corps, under General Mouton, to sustain his troops, and finally to break the English line, when he receives the news of the attack by the Prussians, and that d'Homond's corps is not sufficient to keep them back. Napoleon is obliged to send his 6th army corps in this direction, and arrest the advance of the Prussians. It was about four o'clock when this occurred; the battle had raged five hours. The position of the three armies was as follows:—

Up to this hour, Napoleon had only engaged his 1st and 2d army corps; the 6th corps, besides the Guard, had not yet moved, and the greater part of his cavalry had been likewise kept in reserve.

The English, on the other hand, had engaged nearly all their troops; and nearly all their reserves were used up in the action with the two first army corps.

At four o'clock, though nothing is decided, the advance of the 6th corps, supported by the Guards, would have undoubtedly settled the question.

In many parts, the second English line had already entered the first; the loss in killed, wounded, and deserters was exceedingly heavy, and all those remaining had to do their utmost to prevent the 1st and 2d French corps breaking their lines.

Since two o'clock Ney had been deprived of his 3000 horse commanded by General d'Homond; and, just at the moment he should have been assisted by the 6th corps, this was sent to drive back the Prussians. At four o'clock, the Prussians, with 20,000 men, commence their attack. They are first repulsed by the 6th army corps and the cavalry of General d'Homond; but, being continually reinforced by fresh troops, they oblige General Mouton to retreat, and enter

Planchenois at about five o'clock; they are, therefore, in the rear of a part of the French army.

In the mean time, Ney had redoubled his efforts; Haye Sainte, Papelotte, and Haye are in his undisputed possession.

At Papelotte the fight is recommenced in favor of the English by the arrival of Prussian troops. To aid his further attacks, Ney orders the advance of the cavalry of General Guyot.

Those Cuirassiers and Lancers take the English batteries, and force the cannoneers to retreat.

The English infantry forms squares; the French cavalry is forced to retreat to its own lines; Napoleon sends to its assistance the cavalry of Kellermann, and at the same time he is obliged to send a division of the Guards to sustain General Mouton in Planchenois. The Prussians are driven from Planchenois, but, reinforced again, they return to the charge; Napoleon sends another part of the Guards in this direction. The Cuirassiers of Kellermann, in the mean time, attack the enemy's line; his cannoneers retreat; some battalions are cut down; the English infantry forms in squares; the French artillery, which had the greatest difficulty in advancing, is now near enough to commence a destructive fire against the English line; but again, at the decisive moment, Napoleon is obliged to send in another direction the troops which should have supported those different attacks and dealt the final blow.

Wellington has assembled near his center whatever men he could spare from his right and left wings. His loss, at this moment, amounted to 18,000 men killed and disabled;

nearly half this number had deserted, or were employed carrying away the wounded.

Ney attacked the English line so vigorously with his exhausted troops that it was much shaken; the whole of the second line was put in the first, and two fresh divisions, Chassé and division Belge, came forward to support the center.

It was six o'clock; the army corps of Pirsch I. had entered the battle-field, and repulsed the French right wing near Papelotte.

Ziethen's army corps had arrived on the left of Planchenois, and, with Bülow, attacked this village. Napoleon, unaware of these facts, wished to strike the last blow. With one division of the Old Guard, all that was left for reserve, he arranged the attack on the left side of the main road; Ney and Reille were to assemble whatever men they could, and advance simultaneously with him.

It is seven o'clock, and this last attack on the English line is made.

Wellington, seeing their advance, arranges several battalions from the right wing in second line, and keeps the division Chassé in reserve. The 4th and 6th brigades of cavalry were brought from the left wing.

The whole French line was in movement.

The Guard's advance was supported by four batteries.

The English batteries fired only at the advancing battalions.

The Brunswick battalions, which first presented themselves to the French Guard, were repulsed.

Wellington ordered the advance of the six battalions he

had kept in reserve; they received the Guard with a murderous fire. A moment the column stopped, and only a moment; it advanced again; the first English line was broken, and a battery carried.

The Guard deployed at a short distance from the second English line; it was assailed by a horrible fire, which it returned at only a few yards' distance. At this moment, the Prussian reserve artillery, conducted by Pirsch I., opened its fire on the right flank of the advancing column; this, together with the obstinate resistance of the English in the center, and the want of fresh troops on the French side to sustain the attack, caused the Guard to retreat. Its loss was heavy. This was the moment for the English line to advance. The Prussians, on the other hand, pressed forward from the wing.

The retreating French battalions soon found themselves turned and surrounded; they disbanded on all sides; their efforts in the attack had occasioned this disorder, and no reserve was present to stop the enemy's advance, and to give them time to rally.

Planchenois was taken by the Prussians, who now occupied the French line of retreat.

The retreat becomes at every moment more disorderly; the cavalry of the allies charges whatever presents itself, and very soon all order and discipline cease—cavalry, artillery, infantry, all pell mell, try to get beyond the reach of the pursuers. Only two or three batteries were saved.

Blücher's cavalry pursued the enemy during the whole night as far as Charleroi.

In this memorable battle, the English had to contend

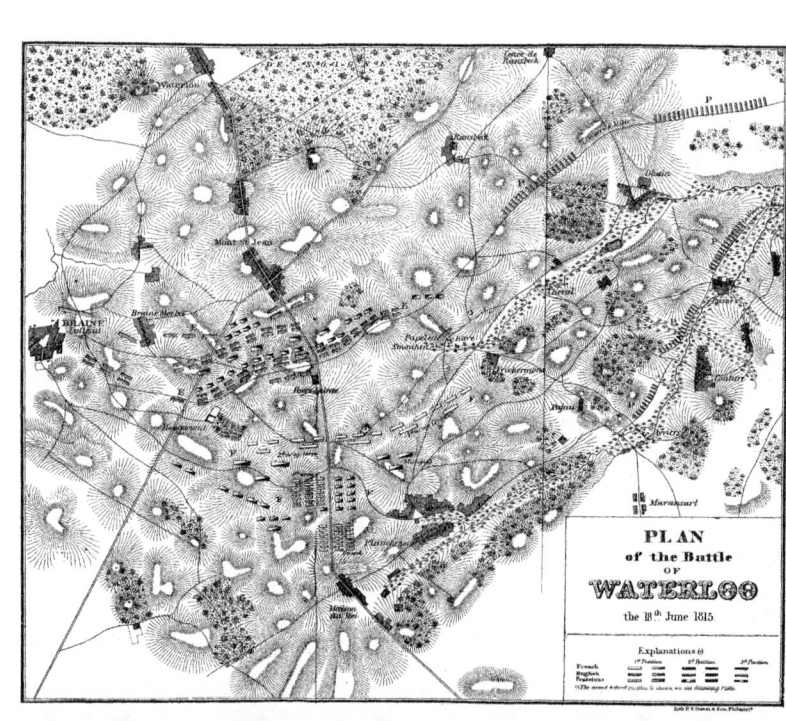

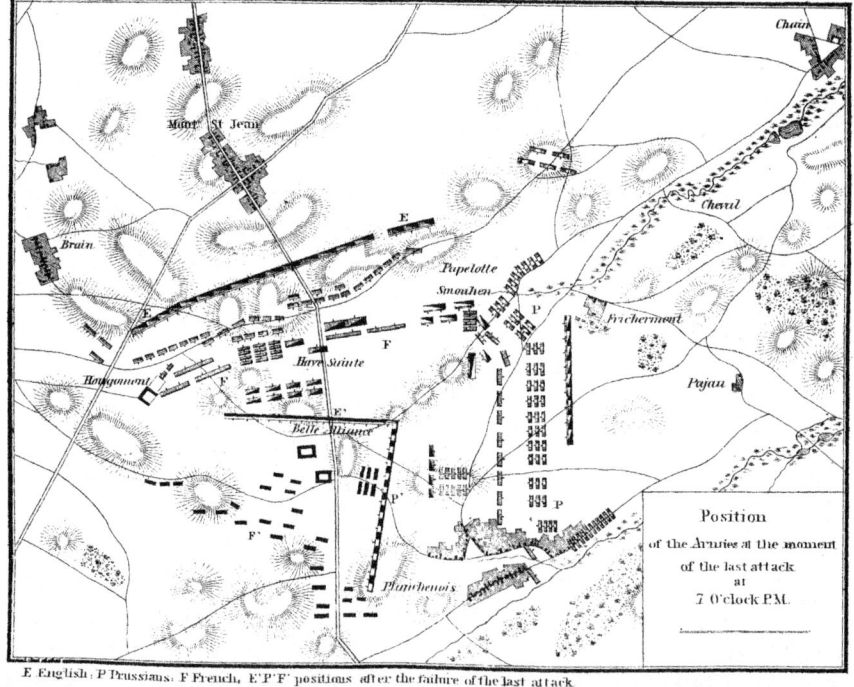

E English, P Prussians, F French, E'P'F' positions after the failure of the last attack.

GRAND TACTICS.   149

with 55 of the French battalions, and the Prussians with 42; these last, however, were Napoleon's best troops, consisting of nearly all the Guard and of the 6th corps, which had not been present, and consequently had not experienced any loss, at the battles of Ligny and Quatre-Bras.

The loss of the English amounted to 21,000 men; that of the Prussians, to 7000. The French estimate their total loss, at Ligny, Quatre-Bras, and Waterloo, at from 25,000 to 30,000 men. The result of this battle would evidently have been very different, if the English, instead of being attacked by 40,000 French only, had been attacked also by the remaining 30,000 men, who did not fire a single round against them.

MIXED OPERATIONS.

SEVERAL operations, in a war, belong partly to Strategy and partly to Tactics—such as Passage of Rivers, Retreats and Descents. It is therefore necessary to say a few words concerning them.

PASSAGE OF RIVERS.

In the passage of a river, we distinguish—
1st. The point where we intend passing it.
2d. The operation of the passage.

The first example of strategy, War in the United States, is sufficient to show of what importance is the point of passage over a large river.

Different passages of the Potomac, Mississippi, Ohio, and Missouri are discussed there; it is shown how different the result would be, if, instead of crossing, for instance, the Mississippi at Memphis, it was crossed at Cairo.

If we have but one point where we can cross the river, and if our only line of retreat leads through this point, it must be fortified; the fort, called the tête-de-pont, should be large enough to hold at least a part of our army.

The more the bridge is of importance, the stronger the fortifications should be.

As regards tactical arrangements for the passage of a river in the presence of an enemy, we may say—

1st. It is necessary to deceive the enemy concerning the real point of passage.

We should make demonstrations, feint attacks, and trials of passage on different points, with much noise, in order to attract the enemy's attention.

The greatest silence should be kept on the real point of passage, and the operations should be conducted with the utmost speed.

2d. The construction of the bridge must, in many cases, be facilitated by sending troops in boats to the other side, to prevent the enemy's skirmishers molesting our men while at work.

3d. Strong batteries, of heavy caliber, should be placed in position, to hinder any artillery of the enemy being placed in like manner on the opposite side; the banks on our side should therefore slightly overlook those on the enemy's.

4th. Large islands in rivers offer many advantages, as well as small streams flowing near the point of a passage in the main river, to place our boats and make our arrangements out of the enemy's sight.

5th. It would be well to choose a place where the river forms a curve, to be able to protect our troops by our artillery.

Fig. 30.

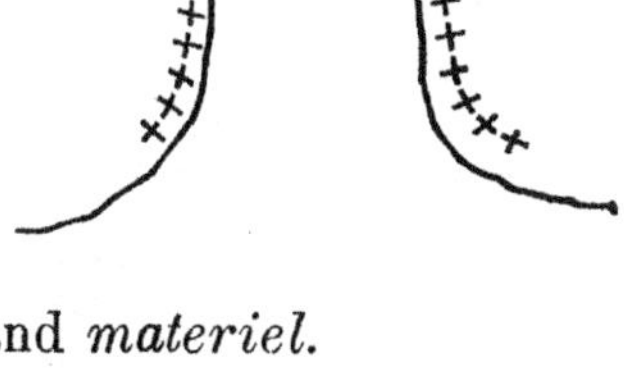

6th. There should be good roads near the passage, to permit of an easy arrival of the men and *materiel*.

To defend the passage of a river, the greatest care should

be taken to have all the different points well watched; at short distances smaller corps of observation should be disposed, in order to arrest for a short time the passage, or at least the forming of a bridge. These corps place sentries along the river so as to form a continuous chain, and, in case of an attempt to cross, to give the alarm from one end of our line to the other.

A good ordnance or telegraph service should be organized, too.

The main force that defends the passage should form two or three corps, disposed so that they can easily join and render assistance to each other, and arrive in time at the endangered point.

There are two ways to act against an army passing a river.

The first is, to hinder the forming of a bridge and the passage of the enemy at the very onset of his operation.

The second is, to allow a part of the enemy's army to pass without hinderance, and then attack it with a superior force, and try to defeat it.

Either of these two ways can be chosen according to circumstances, as shown in the following cases:—

In the campaign of 1799, the Archduke Charles tried the passage of the Aar at Dettingen. He had disposed a formidable artillery on the right bank of the river, but, having no small boats, was unable to send one or two battalions to the opposite side, to keep the enemy's sharpshooters at a distance, before the bridge was commenced.

Opposed only by a few companies of riflemen hidden among the bushes and in the houses, they fired at and killed most of the men engaged in the forming of the bridge, and hindered its completion till assistance arrived to render the passage impossible.

In the campaigns of the Prince Eugene, this general, opposed to General Vendôme, tried to pass the Adda in a very favorable spot, after having gained a march on the French general. Vendôme, however, being timely informed, arrived in all haste; the bridge was already commenced, and he could not prevent its being finished.

He ordered, therefore, some field-works to be raised in a large circle round the spot where the bridge was built; this was done simultaneously by his whole army, and finished at the same time as the bridge. The Prince Eugene, thinking now the passage of his troops too dangerous to be undertaken, gave up his plan.

In 1809, Napoleon crossed the Danube from the Isle of Lobau; when a part of his army only had passed, the Austrians loosened large ships laden with stones, and had them driven against the bridge, which was broken.

In the mean time, the Archduke Charles had attacked the French army with his own superior force, and, after a murderous fight which lasted all day, and in which the villages of Esslingen and Aspern were taken and retaken, the French, after enormous losses, were obliged to retreat. In this battle the Austrians lost about 20,000, and the French 25,000 men. The greatest loss they sustained at the end of the battle, when their troops, forming a convex line, were exposed to a concentric fire of artillery from the Austrians.

For acting in a similar way, it is necessary that the right

moment should not be lost, and not to permit too many troops to pass before the attack is made.

At Consarbruck, the French general, Crequi, allowed the enemy to pass purposely, to attack him when the half of his army had gained the other side. The passage commenced, but Crequi hesitated to attack. When asked why he did not begin, he replied, that the more that passed, the more would be beaten. At last he attacked; but the enemy had already assembled in such strength that he himself was totally routed.

Finally, there is one way more to render a passage ineffectual, which we may follow. It is, to cross the river ourselves as soon as the enemy does.

In 1674, Montecuculi crossed the Rhine to make war in France. Turenne, who was opposed to him, instead of defending the French territory, crossed himself this river, and commenced operations in Germany, and by this forced Montecuculi's return.

The following example will show in detail how the passage of a river might be conducted :—

EXAMPLE.

PASSAGE OF THE LIMMAT BY MASSENA, 1799.

In 1799, the Archduke Charles, with an Austrian army, was opposed by General Massena; their two armies were separated by the Lake of Zurich, the Limmat, and the Aar. The Archduke was called back to Germany; but he left

General Kutusoff, with 27,000 men, in Zurich and its environs. Suwaroff, coming from Italy, was to join Kutusoff. Massena, being informed of the allies' plan, took the decision to pass to the offensive, to defeat Kutusoff before he could make his intended junction with Suwaroff. To effect this, he was obliged to cross the Limmat; and he therefore made the necessary arrangements to do so near Dietikon.

The division of Soult had orders to pass the Lynth between the Lake of Zurich and that of Wallenstadt; a part of the division of Menard was to make a demonstration on the Limmat below Dietikon and near the junction with the River Aar.

The Limmat near Dietikon forms a large curve; from Giessäker to Kl. Fahr the distance is 2000 yards.

A small river, the Schäfflibach, runs into the Limmat almost in the middle of the curve.

Opposite the Schäfflibach is a little wood, called the Glanzenberg; about 250 yards from which is a hill covered by another wood, called the Hardt-holz.

The space between the two woods is a meadow, and could be easily reached and swept by the batteries A and B. The battery B overlooked completely the opposite bank of the river. The bridge was to be established just below the Schäfflibach and behind the wood Glanzenberg, so that it was protected from the fire of artillery; this wood, then, would form a kind of tête-de-pont.

The Limmat, at the point of passage, measures 100 yards wide; no isles or confluents were near this point, to serve as cover to the boats for the bridge as well as for the passage, and they would therefore be obliged to be launched out of sight of the enemy.

The technical arrangements for the passage were left to Colonel Dedon, of the Engineers. He had in his possession 16 regulation pontoons, with all the accessories; they were at Lunnern, forming a bridge there over the Reuss, and were to be transported by land to Dietikon. Besides the pontoons, 37 boats, of different dimensions, could be had, the larger capable of containing 45, the smaller ones 20 armed infantry soldiers; they were also to be transported a great distance by land.

The passage was to take place on the morning of the 25th of September, and the pontoons started only in the night of the 23d to the 24th from Lunnern to Dietikon.

The position of the Russians, on the right bank of the Limmat, was as follows :—

The right wing, General Durasoff, 8 battalions and 10 squadrons, or 6000 men, placed near Wettingen and Würenlos; 3 battalions and 400 Cossacks, or 2400 men, under General Markoff, were placed near the spot chosen by Massena; their position is shown in the plan.

Near Höngg 1000 cavalry were stationed.

The extreme left was formed by a reserve of 3000 men near Schwamendingen.

The headquarters of Kutusoff were in Zurich.

Two corps, composed of 5600 men, under General Gortschakoff, were placed on the left side of the Limmat, between Wollishofen and Siehfeld.

3000 men were near Kloten; the remaining 5000 men were opposed to Soult on the upper part of the Lake of Zurich.

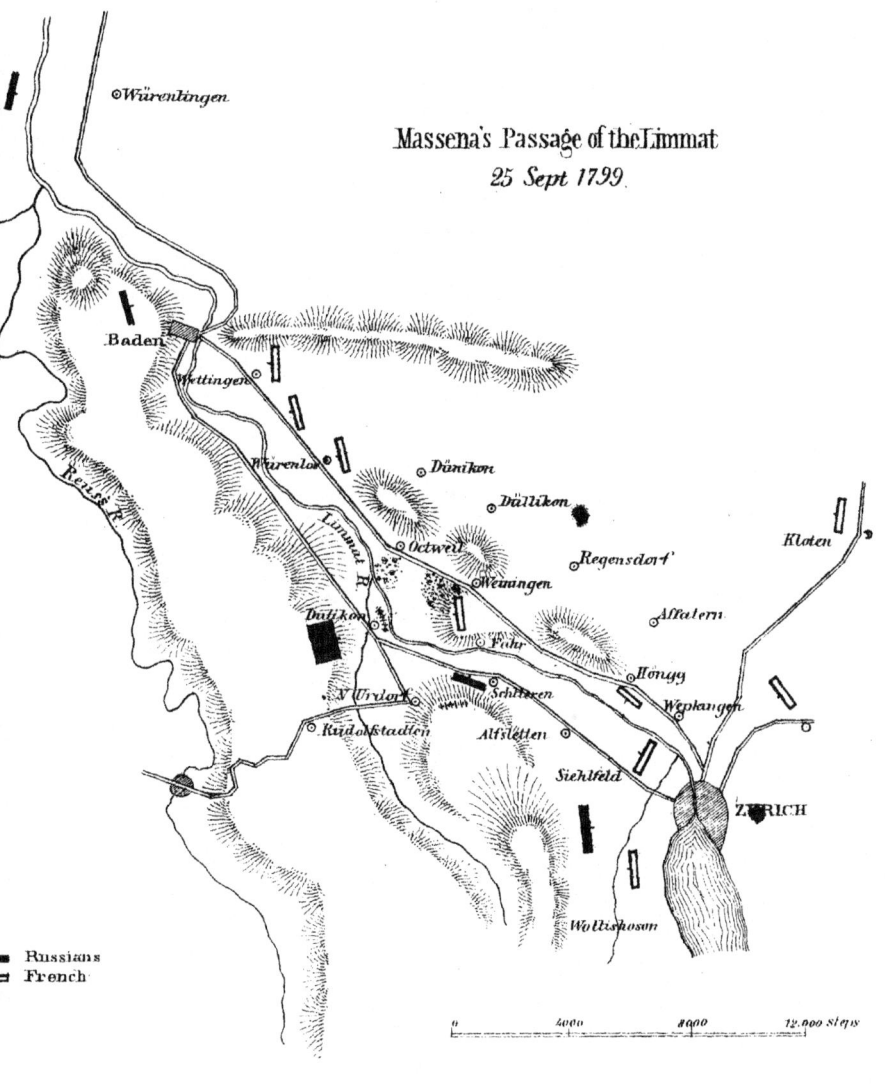

The Russians had disposed many pickets along the Limmat, and had placed a sentry at nearly every 100 yards.

The position of the French was:—

The division of Mortier, 6000 men, opposed to General Gortschakoff.

The 5th division, General Lorges, 12,000 men, distributed from Schlieren to Baden.

The 6th division, General Menard, 8000 men, at Baden and on the lower banks of the river.

The reserve, division of Klein, in the Frickthal.

The dispositions for the passage were—

1st. The division of Lorges and part of the division of Menard, in all 16,000 men, were to cross the Limmat at Dietikon—the Engineers commanded by Colonel Dedon, and the Artillery by Chef d'Escadron Foy.

2d. As soon as the passage had been forced, General Lorges was to leave a strong detachment opposed to the Russian right wing under General Durasoff, and with his main body to march by Fahr and Höngg toward Zurich, to cut off the retreat of the Russian left wing under General Gortschakoff.

3d. General Menard, with his remaining troops, was to demonstrate near Baden, and to draw the attention of the 6000 Russians under General Durasoff on him, while the real passage took place at Dietikon.

4th. To prevent General Gortschakoff attacking the rear of the passing divisions, General Mortier was to attack him on the morning of the 25th.

5th. General Klein was to station himself, with 4000 troops of the reserve division and cavalry, near Schlieren, to be able to render assistance at any point where it should be required.

Without counting the 3000 Russians at Kloten, four or five miles distant, Massena, with 30,000 men, opposes 18,000; of these, 6000 are occupied on the right wing by a demonstration; 5600, under Gortschakoff, are paralyzed by Mortier's attack; so that, in fact, the main attack of Massena is executed with 20,000 against 6400.

Passage.

On the night of the 24th, General Lorges, with his 16,000 men, noiselessly assembled near Dietikon.

Colonel Dedon had three and a half companies of Engineers, two and a half of which were ordered to bring the boats near the river and man them; the remaining company was to form the bridge.

One battalion and four companies of infantry were likewise put under the command of Colonel Dedon, to assist in the transportation of the boats. These boats had been placed in the rear of Dietikon, in a certain order, and all numbered; they were carried on the men's shoulders to the river, and disposed there in the same order. Some of the boats, being very heavy, required 100 men to transport them; however, this part of the work was performed in the greatest silence, and without anything having been observed by the Russian sentries.

There were three kinds of boats—small, medium, and large. The smallest were to enter the river above, and the largest below; the operation was to commence with the smallest boats.

The bank of the river was from seven to eight feet in height, so that the launching of the boats occasioned some difficulty; a detachment of sappers received orders to arrange planks on an inclined plan, so that the boats could be easily let down. When all was ready, the boats were once more inspected, to see if everything was in order; the men then lay down near them, till the signal was given to begin the passage.

The artillery was arranged in the following manner:—

One battery, B, of 12-pounders, was placed, as shown in the plan, to sweep the country between the two woods; another battery, A, consisting principally of howitzers, was placed so as to be able to shell the barracks of the three Russian battalions placed a little behind the Hardt-holz; finally, a battery of 12-pounders was placed opposite Oetweil, a little beyond, so as to sweep the main road from this place to Würenlos, which is on the right side of the Limmat, and bordered by very steep hills several hundred feet high.

The object in having this battery was to prevent General Durasoff coming to the assistance of Markoff.

These dispositions were made in such silence that even the French troops were unaware of them.

After midnight, the advanced guard, under General Gazan, stationed itself at about 50 yards from the river.

The light boats were at the mouth of the Schäfflibach, which at the time was dried up; these boats could hold about 180 men.

At the dawn of day, orders were given to lower the boats as quietly as possible into the river, for the troops of the advanced guard to enter them, to pass to the other side and occupy the Glanzholz.

The nine light boats were more quickly lowered than the others; the infantry entered them, but being too heavily loaded, some difficulty arose in pushing them from the bank; therefore some of the men were ordered out. The noise this occasioned, though little, was sufficient to put the Russians on the alert. One of the sentries fired; this was repeated by all the others along the river; and the alarm spread through the whole line from Baden to Zurich, and in a few minutes the entire Russian army was under arms.

No time was to be lost; the boats were pushed into the river, manned, and rowed to the other side; and in three minutes from the time the Russian sentry had fired the first shot, 600 French troops had landed in the Glanzenberg, all their batteries had opened fire, and the Russian posts were driven back into the Hardt-holz.

The boats empty, they returned to the left bank, and transported more troops to the other side; and, before the bridge was completed, 8000 men had been carried to the right bank by the boats. Scarcely, however, had they returned from their first expedition when the *general* was beaten on the other side of the river, and as this could come from the 600 French who were ready to advance, as well as from the Russians, the fire on the left bank was ordered to cease, so as not to endanger their own troops by continuing it.

At a quarter to five o'clock the passage began, and half an hour afterward the French were sufficiently strong to attack and drive the Russians from the Hardt-holz; at six o'clock this was accomplished.

The bridge was commenced at five o'clock, and at seven it was finished. A party of sappers had been sent on the right bank to open a road for cavalry and artillery through the Glanzenberg. At half-past seven, the remainder of Lorges' 16,000 men, with their cavalry, crossed the bridge. Two French battalions were directed at Oetweil to arrest the advance of General Durasoff, if he should try to pass on the road to Zurich.

The remainder, about 14,000 men, were arranged in order of battle near Fahr, and at ten o'clock began to advance in the direction of Höngg; after a short fight, General Markoff was again repulsed, and in the course of the afternoon the French advanced as far as Wipkingen and Schwamendingen.

In the morning, Mortier had attacked General Gortschakoff with the greatest impetuosity, and had succeeded in driving him toward Zurich.

Kutusoff, thinking this was the main attack, called the 3000 reserves from Schwamendingen, and, with their help, Mortier was in turn repulsed.

It was only in the afternoon, when Massena had arrived at the gates of Zurich, and even summoned Kutusoff to surrender, that the latter felt all the danger of his position; he called in his reserve, and, with the assistance of some of the battalions arrived from the 5000 men opposed to Soult, he was enabled to repulse Massena, forcing him back as far as Wipkingen. General Klein, in the mean time, with his reserve, advanced on the left side of the Limmat to support Mortier, and they forced General Gortschakoff to fall back on Zurich.

General Menard's demonstration on the left wing had

been very successful. To deceive the Russians as to his strength, he disposed his troops in single ranks, and made several attempts to cross the river, which he even accomplished in some parts.

In consequence of this, Durasoff advanced still farther down the Limmat, leaving the decisive point behind him; when he discovered his mistake, he endeavored to reach Zurich, and only arrived at a junction with Kutusoff by making a great circuit.

The next day, Kutusoff tried to open himself a passage in the direction of Winterthur; in this attempt he lost a great part of his army.

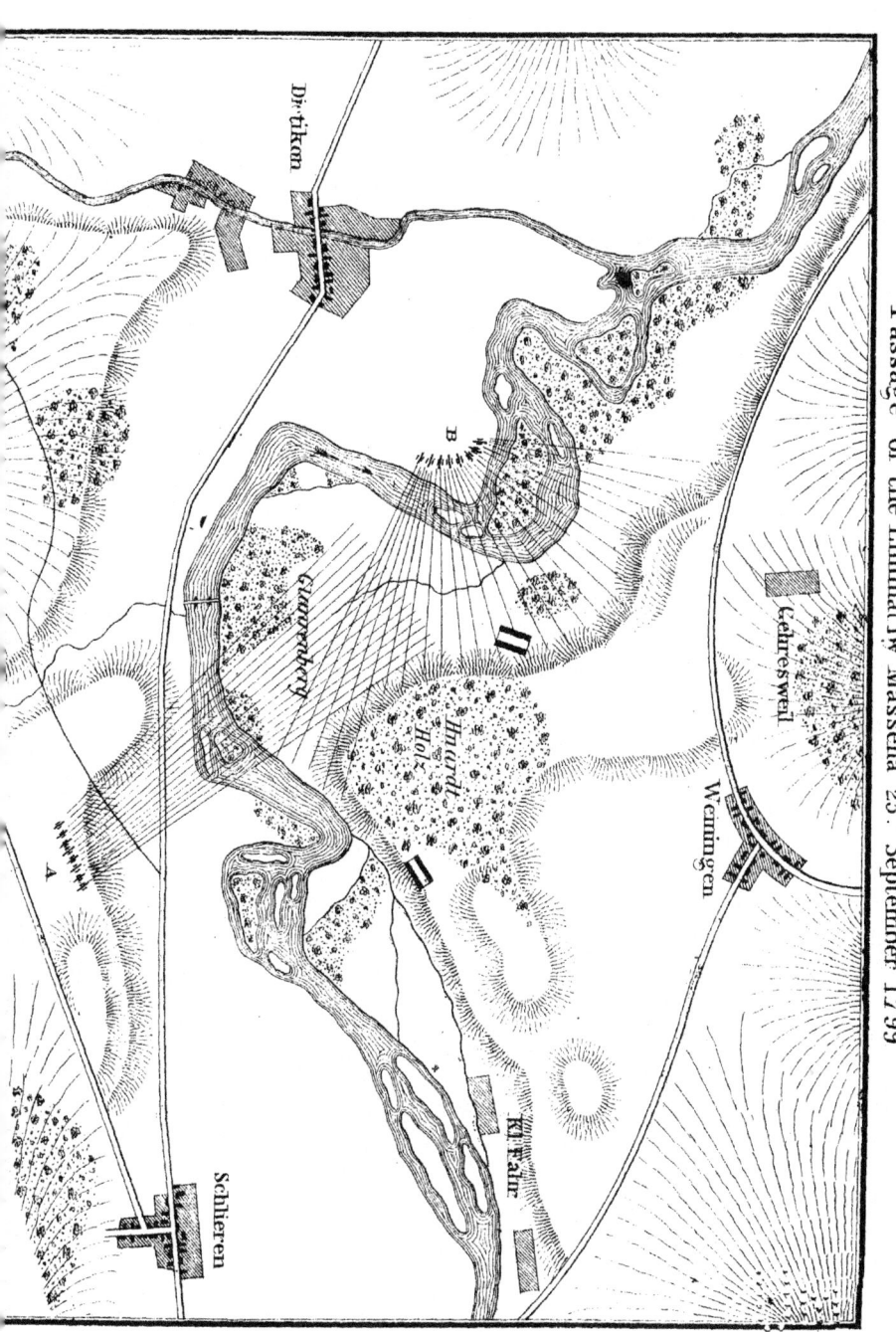

RETREAT AND PURSUIT.

The moment we leave the battle-field to retreat, our operation becomes one of Strategy as well as of Tactics. The direction in which we retreat is of the utmost importance. In the example of the battle of Waterloo this can easily be seen. If Blücher, after the battle of Ligny, had retreated to Namur, as many a general would have done, Wellington's army would have been lost, and a double defeat the consequence; his retreat to Wavre, and arrival at Belle Alliance, changed the defeat to the most decided victory.

The direction of our retreat will depend on many circumstances.

If we are co-operating with another army, we should retreat in this direction, to make a junction with it and obtain a central position between the enemy's armies. We may also retreat directly into the heart of our country; or we may retreat parallel to the frontiers. In the first example we have already spoken of this last.

The reasons for our retreat may be different, likewise. We may retreat after a lost battle, as did Jordan, for instance, in 1796, and Napoleon in 1813, when driven back from the Bohemian frontiers across the Rhine; or before a very superior enemy, as the Russians did in 1812 before Napoleon; or in consequence of a preconcerted strategical plan, as in the campaign of the Archduke Charles in 1796; or, in consequence of strategical movements of the enemy, to keep free our lines of communication—the retreat of Moreau in 1796 was such. We may also retreat to gain a favorable position for a battle, as did Napoleon before the battle of Austerlitz; and, finally, to approach nearer our depots and magazines, if we are in a devastated country—such was the reason of Napoleon's retreat in the Russian campaign.

The arrangements for a retreating army belong more to logistics than to tactics; and to well understand them, it is necessary first to read the chapter on logistics. I will only give the principal moments, and the rest will be found in the next chapter.

So long as a retreating army is not pursued, its march offers nothing particular; but from the moment the enemy is in pursuit, the question changes entirely; and it becomes most difficult after a lost battle.

Small armies, in which disorder can never be so very great, should try to evade pursuit by forced or night marches; but with large armies this is impossible—a slow and well-ordered retreat must be executed, with strong rear guards. The service of the latter being very difficult, they are relieved every twenty-four hours; that is, the main body, arrived at a favorable place for defense, leaves a number of troops equal to the rear guard; these form in line of battle, and receive the rear guard, which now retreats, and joins the main body. The new rear guard arrests as long as possible the progress of the enemy's advanced guard, and then begins its own retreat. In large armies, the rear guard is generally com-

MIXED OPERATIONS.

posed of a whole army corps. In most cases, it amounts to one-third of the entire force.

As regards the disposition of the retreating columns, there are several: We may march our whole army on one road and in one mass, or on one road but in several columns, separated by one or several days' march; or we may retreat on several parallel roads, or on divergent or concentric lines.

Retreats on divergent lines are to be rejected; those on concentric ones, to be recommended. As regards the three other modes, we can only say this—that, in the march for retreat as well as in that for advance, our army must be always so arranged that it can form from the marching order as quickly as possible in line of battle, or at least be able to bring, in a fight, at the same time as the enemy, a force equal to his own.

If the enemy pursues us having his army formed in one long column on one road, we might retreat in a similar way, or even in leaving a space of from one-half to one day's march between the columns, to prevent the incumbrance of the roads.

Retreats in one column have the great disadvantage of leading us very easily into difficulties by the incumbrance of the roads, which occasions the stopping of the whole army.

If the enemy pursues us disposed in several columns marching parallel, we would be obliged to do the same, as, by not doing so, our rear guard would risk being separated from the army by the flank columns of the enemy.

Finally, if pursued on our flank, our arrangements must be similar to a flank march, the disposition of which is given under Logistics.

The rear guard, according to its importance, should be several miles to half a day's march from the main army.

The commanding officer should be most intrepid and enterprising, and at the same time cool and steady. He should more often and more impetuously attack the advanced guard of the pursuing enemy than allow himself to be attacked; this sustains the *morale* of the troops, and renders the enemy slower and less bold in his pursuit.

On the other hand, the pursuit should be conducted with the greatest energy and most unceasing activity, so as not to give the retreating army time to form again and reorganize.

Pursuits on the flank, if in our own country, are more advantageous than those in the rear, as they enable the pursuing army to prevent the retreat at the passage of a river or at any place it chooses to do so.

At the retreat of Napoleon in the Russian campaign, the Russian army marched parallel with him on his flank; it arrived before him at Krasnoi, and only by a miracle he saved part of his army. The passage of the Beresina, in this same retreat, shows how dangerous it is, when the army is obliged to cross a river in the presence of, and opposed by, the pursuing enemy.

If we retreat in consequence of a strategical movement and are pursued by an inferior enemy, as was Moreau in 1796, we should act like him—that is, to disengage our rear by trying to engage and defeat the pursuer. General Latour, with only 30,000 men, was imprudent enough to accept the battle offered to him by Moreau with 50,000 men. Latour was defeated at Biberach, on the 2d of October, 1796; after his victory, Moreau continued his retreat unmolested.

DESCENTS AND EXPEDITIONS.

HERE, again, we must consider the strategical and the tactical arrangement. Descents are undertaken for the conquest of a country or an island; or they have only a restricted object, such as the destruction of arsenals, depots, ships, etc. etc. of an enemy; or, finally, they are made to serve as a diversion.

If the object of an expedition is the conquest of a country, the first thing necessary is to see that its means are sufficient.

If acting against an uncivilized nation, which has no regular army, or at least without such armed and disciplined men as our own, the result of such a descent is generally a favorable one. The conquest of India by the English, of Egypt and Algiers by the French, and the expedition by these powers united against China, are examples of this.

For descents on islands, we have but to look at English history for examples. James, in his excellent naval history, gives a detailed description of all those made during the wars of the French revolution and empire.

On the other hand, expeditions against a civilized country are attended with the greatest difficulties and danger. The English armies in the United States are a proof of this, and the Peninsular war might likewise serve as an example. If we look at Moore's retreat to Corunna in 1809, and at Murray's expedition to Tarragona, we will see all the dangers arising from such enterprises. The English could never have succeeded in conquering the Peninsula, had they not been assisted by the population of the whole country.

Expeditions with a restricted object, but still of a certain extent, are scarcely ever attended with the results we anticipate; or, at least, what we obtain by them is seldom an equivalent for the cost. Examples of this are the English expedition to Antwerp in 1809, and the great expedition to the Crimea in 1854.

To understand this, the reader must be well impressed with the principles of strategy. An expedition is nothing else than a large detachment, or a division of our force separated from us by exterior lines. If this detachment has a light task only to perform—such as the burning of undefended or slightly defended magazines, depots, and towns, or the destruction of some coast batteries, etc.—it is, in most cases, successful; that is, if the arrangements have been well planned, and the secret of the expedition well kept. In these cases, the means are small, and no great preparation necessary. If, on the contrary, the detachment has a certain rôle to play—such as acting against the enemy's rear, to force him to make detachments, to take possession of places, and, in one word, after its disembarkation, to execute an offensive operation in the country—its task becomes difficult.

These operations are then generally successful at the commencement, because the enemy is unable to have strong forces on every point of his coast; but, knowing once the point attacked, he can easily concentrate greater forces, and not only defeat, but utterly destroy these detachments as soon as they leave the protection of their ships.

In expeditions serving only as diversions, it would be much better to have but one detachment, which is quickly transported from one place to another, making descents near the larger towns, forcing them to pay contributions, and thereby obliging the enemy to a large display of force on his coasts. Those troops are lost to him; he cannot make any use of them, in the continual expectation of being attacked. On the other hand, we oppose to all his forces only that one, but continually changing detachment, which descends everywhere excepting on or near the point where the enemy awaits it. In such a way more is gained than by half a dozen expeditions, which would only conduct us to a division of our own forces, and draw them from the decisive point.

The tactical arrangements for a descent are very similar to those for the passage of a river.

We must distinguish the case of the descent being opposed or not. In the last case, speed is the principal requisition; the troops should disembark as quickly as possible, before the enemy can appear. The vessels of war which accompany these expeditions should be disposed on the right and left sides of the descending troops, so as to sweep the country with their heavy guns. Necks of land entering the sea are most favorable for the disembarkation, as they permit of a concentric fire from the ships, and the possibility of arranging the troops in good order before advancing, and their retreat in the same space covered by their ships. It is exactly the same as a river forming a curve.

If the descent is to be made on a part where the enemy is in force, it is necessary to deceive him on the real point, to draw his forces in another direction, by making feigned attacks, and by bringing the ships of transport in the night near the chosen point of descent, which should be made at daybreak.

All the large boats should be provided with boat howitzers, similar to those of Captain Dahlgren, for instance, which are of an excellent pattern; they should be landed, and immediately serve as artillery to the troops going on shore, until their own field artillery is landed. The disembarkation should be well flanked by the ships of war.

As soon as a sufficient number of troops is assembled, and if the enemy has been totally deceived as to the point of attack, they should advance, without losing time, against the rear or flank of the enemy, who is not prepared for such an attack.

If the landing is only slightly opposed, the troops should also advance as soon as possible to hinder the enemy assembling in too great force to prevent or endanger the disembarkation.

Islands near the main land are very favorable for descents, as the enemy has great difficulty to sustain his force placed there; and, once gained, they offer us a secure base for further operations. As soon as the descent has been made, field-works should be raised to serve as a sort of tête-de-pont. These works should be large enough to hold the greater parts of the troops from the expedition; the depots and magazines should also be established there; they should be situated so as to cover the ships, and enable the troops to re-embark at any moment and in any kind of weather. The fortifications form the base of operation for the landed troops.

The position of Wellington near Lisbon, and the fortifications of Torres Vedras to cover it, are a fine example.

Fig. 31.

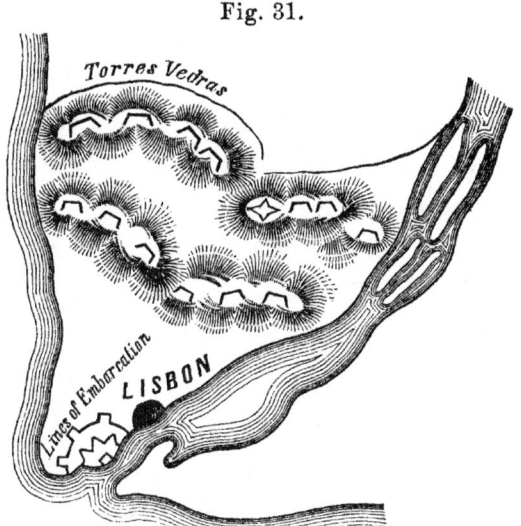

The country in this part forms a triangle; on one side is the sea, on the other the Tagus, and the third side formed the fortifications of Torres Vedras, so called from the village of this name. The Tagus was an excellent port for English vessels; and the peninsula which was formed by it and the sea was large enough to hold any army.

The most difficult and dangerous part, however, for a corps in an expedition, is its advance, or when ordered to operate in the interior of a country.

The Peninsular war is an excellent study for all such enterprises.

A few words on the defense may find their place here.

It is seldom possible to effectually oppose a descent; but

when accomplished, the disembarking corps should be crushed by superior armies.

The most certain way would be to oppose it but little; to leave a corps of observation at the point of descent, which retreats before the corps of the expedition. But as soon as it is at a certain distance from its base, it should be attacked by very superior forces, and by means of tactical manœuvres be entirely separated from its base.

In trying to cut off its line of retreat by strategical manœuvres, the corps we intend to act against might be informed in time of our movements, and quickly retreat to its base; we would then gain nothing. The result of a fight in which the corps is outflanked and turned by a superior force is, therefore, to be preferred.

The corps of observation left opposed to the expedition should throw up some field-works in opposition to those of the latter, so as to render its advance, at least, not entirely without danger. It should also defend the passage of rivers, defiles, etc.

LOGISTICS.

It would be much too long, in a summary like this, to give all the details concerning the different operations of Logistics. This branch forms one of the special studies of the officers of the General Staff. General Jomini, in his treatise on the Art of War, gives, as belonging to Logistics, the following :—

1st. To prepare beforehand all the necessary *materiel* for the opening of the campaign. Draw up the orders and instructions for the assemblage of the army and its being put in movement.

2d. To draw up the orders of the General-in-Chief for the different enterprises, as well as the plans of attack for premeditated fights.

3d. To concert with the chiefs of Artillery and Engineers the measures to be taken for the safety of the different depots and magazines.

4th. To command and direct the reconnoitering parties, and to procure by any means information concerning the enemy.

5th. To take the necessary measures for the combination of the different movements ordered by the General-in-Chief. To prepare the march for the different columns, that it may be executed with order and *ensemble*. To render the march easy and safe, and to regulate the time for halting.

6th. To compose and direct by good instructions the advanced and rear guards, as well as detached corps. To supply them with every necessary to fulfill their duties.

7th. To fix the instructions of each commander of an army corps for the arrangement and composition of his columns on arriving near the enemy, as well as their arrangement and distribution in line of battle according to the nature of the ground and the character of the enemy we have to deal with.

8th. To point out to advanced guards and other detached corps the place for reassembling in case of defeat.

9th. To order and survey the march of the trains of artillery, ammunition, provision, etc. etc., and to place them near the troops, but in a way that they do not hinder their movements. To take the necessary measures for order and safety both in marching and resting.

10th. To arrange the successive arrivals of ammunition and provision as soon as they are required; to collect all the means of transport in the country, and regulate its employment.

11th. To adopt the establishment of camps, and regulations for their order, safety, and police.

12th. To establish and organize the lines of operation and the halting-places of the army, as well as the communication of the detached corps with this line. To appoint capable officers to organize and command the rear of the army, to watch over the safety of the detachments and convoys, to give them good instructions, and to see that the means of communication between the base of operation and the army are kept up.

13th. To organize on this line the depots, magazines, hospitals, and workshops, and to provide for their safety.

14th. To keep an account of all the detachments formed either on the flanks or rear of the army; to see to their safety, and give them a place for action.

15th. To unite in companies or battalions all the small troops or isolated men going from the army to the base of operation, or from this to the army.

16th. In a siege, to order and superintend the service of the troops in the trenches.

17th. To take, in a retreat, all possible measures for order; to appoint troops to replace those of the rear guard; to provide for the moving of the trains, so that nothing may be lost, and that they can proceed without any impediment and in the greatest safety.

18th. To assign, in cantonments, positions to the different corps, and indicate to each division a place of assembly in case of alarm; to take all measures for the carrying out of orders, instructions, and regulations.

We must, however, speak of marches as far as their general arrangement is concerned, because from the march we might be obliged to pass to a battle, and then our dispositions should be such that all our troops are able to form speedily in line of battle.

We distinguish four kinds of marches—march in *advance*, in *retreat*, *flank* march, and *manœuvre* march.

The two first can be executed in one column marching on one road, or in several columns marching on several roads. The third requires the formation of at least two parallel columns; in the fourth, the operations are always executed with many columns—if not, it offers nothing different from the three first marches.

The precautions for security which are taken in all these marches emanate from one great rule, which is, *that they should always be, so that the main body has time to form the marching column in line of battle before the enemy can arrive near it.*

All columns on a march should therefore be provided with advanced and rear guards, as well as with detachments to cover the flanks. The distance between these guards and the main body must be regulated by the time this one requires to form in line of battle.

If, for instance, we suppose that our column is one mile in length, the troops in the rear would require about twenty-five minutes to form from the rear of the column in line of battle; the advanced guard should, therefore, be at the distance of about one and a half miles. The advanced guard is generally one-fifth of the main body; it sends out another guard, consisting of about one-sixth of its force, and at a distance permitting the main body of the advanced guard to form in line of battle. This first corps sends out pickets in advance and on the flanks; these are composed, for the most part, of cavalry, which is better able to survey the country, and make its reports quicker. In a march for advance, the rear guard is used only to keep order and cover the trains; it is, therefore, less strong than the advanced guard.

In a retreat, it is the rear guard that is made strongest. Fig. 5, Plate V., shows the disposition of an army corps of five brigades marching in advance.

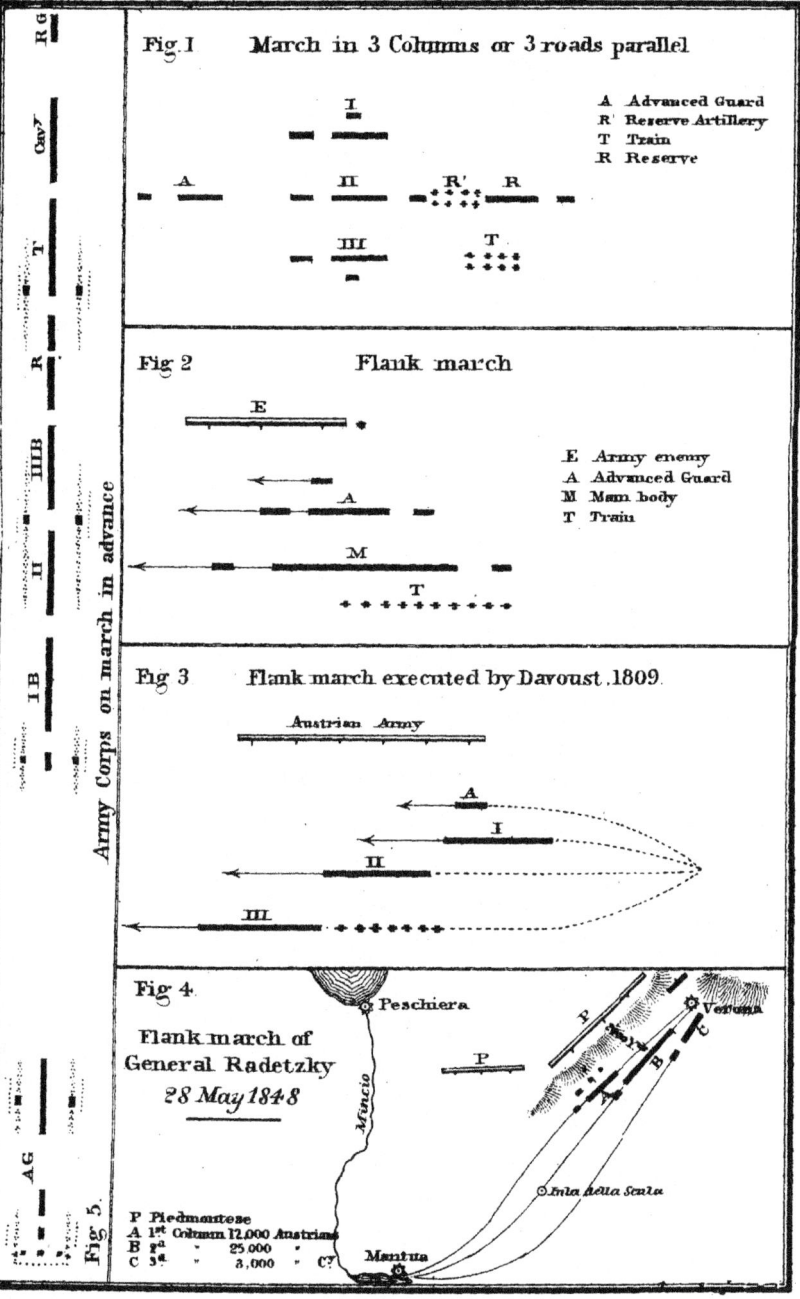

The guard nearest the enemy should be always composed of the three arms.

The artillery belonging to each brigade marches in the center of this brigade; the reserve artillery is generally disposed after the third brigade; then comes the infantry of reserve, then the trains, and, finally, the cavalry, which always marches at the end of the column, it being always able to arrive in time on the battle-field. In marching, a column of 25,000 to 30,000 men occupies a space of 7000 to 8000 yards, without counting the distance from the advanced guard; it is, therefore, evident that large armies can never act or move on one road only.

The different army corps march on different parallel roads; but here again they must be disposed in such a manner that they can with facility form in line, either separately or with the other corps combined. Each of these corps must march just as if it alone were advancing against the enemy; but the distance between all these corps should be such that they can all unite in time. They have a common advanced guard, which marches at a sufficient distance to permit of the other corps joining, and forming in line of battle; and in the same way they have their common rear guard or reserve. Fig. 1, Plate V., shows this disposition.

Flank Marches.

In these marches we present the enemy our flank, and special dispositions must be taken to cover it. Here the advanced guard becomes flank guard, and the whole army is disposed as shown in Fig. 2, Plate V. The greatest necessity exists that good order should be maintained. The trains and baggage are always the most distant from the enemy; the corps should be near enough to be able to render each other prompt assistance. The battalions in the marching columns must be at the necessary distance for deployment, or, in general, to form in line of battle without disorder.

If the army is large, so that several corps may be formed, they should be disposed as shown in Figs. 3 or 4, Plate V.

If the enemy attacks the advanced guard, he offers his own flank to the corps already more advanced or still behind.

Davoust, while retreating from Ratisbon, before the battles of Abensberg, Eckmuhl, etc., formed in a similar way; he executed his march between the Austrian force and the Danube. The flank march of General Radetski, in 1848, from Verona to Mantua, is also remarkable.

By manœuvre marches we understand marches executed by large armies, and having more of a strategical object than a tactical one; they are, in fact, strategical flank marches.

I will give the dispositions for marching as used by Napoleon at Ulm in 1805, and at Jena in 1806. Each of the corps designated in the plan was of three divisions, and in the manœuvres at Ulm that of Ney was of five. In these marches the force of each army corps, and the distance between them, are such that it can resist the enemy's army long enough, till sustained by the others nearest to it.

EXAMPLES.

MARCH AND MANŒUVRES OF NAPOLEON NEAR JENA, 1806.

THE operations near Jena were the following :—

The Prussian army, numbering 120,000 men, was thus disposed: 20,000 near Eisenach, 50,000 near Erfurth, and 50,000 men near Blankenhain.

Napoleon's army was near Bamberg, and amounted to from 170,000 to 180,000 men.

Napoleon determined to cut the Prussians entirely from their base of operation. For this, he advanced in three columns—one in the direction from Coburg to Sahlfeld, another at Kronach and Sahlburg, and a third at Hof and Plauen.

The extreme left of the Prussians was at Schleitz. It was outflanked by the last column, and repulsed by the column in the center.

On the 12th the greater part of the army arrived at Gera, and on the 13th, in the evening, the different army corps occupied the following positions :—

General Angereau at Kahla, 10 miles from Jena, and 7 from Ney, who was at Rohda, 9 miles from Jena; Lannes at Jena; the Guard followed Lannes; Soult on a parallel road to Jena, about 10 miles from this place, and 6 to 7 from the Guard; Davoust, Bernadotte, and Murat arrive at Naumburg, from whence Bernadotte has to march, on the 14th, to Dornburg, and Davoust to Apolda. A part of the cavalry is still at Auma, and the Bavarian division is left at

Plauen to cover the French right flank. Naumburg is about 18 miles from Jena.

If we consider this disposition, we shall find that it answers nearly every case. The Prussian army is entirely separated from its base, and all the corps are so disposed that they can easily assist each other. Lannes forms the advanced guard of the whole army, and, by his arrival in front of the Prussians, keeps them in their position till Davoust arrives at Naumburg. If the Prussians attack him, their loss only becomes more certain, as the decisive point is Naumburg. The result of these marches and manœuvres was the total loss of the Prussian army.

MARCH AND MANŒUVRE OF NAPOLEON NEAR ULM, 1805.

The Austrian general, Mack, with from 70,000 to 80,000 men, advanced from the Austrian frontier as far as Ulm.

Napoleon's army, arriving from Würzburg, Mayence, Spire, and Kehl, numbered 180,000 men. This army was not directed against Ulm, but against the lower towns on the Danube.

The arrangement of the columns is similar to that on a flank march. Ney formed the flank guard, and Soult the advanced guard; the different corps were from 5 to 10 miles distant from each other, and the whole front of operations was from 45 to 50 miles in length.

Wherever Mack attacks, he finds the corps he attacks always supported, in less than three hours, by two or three

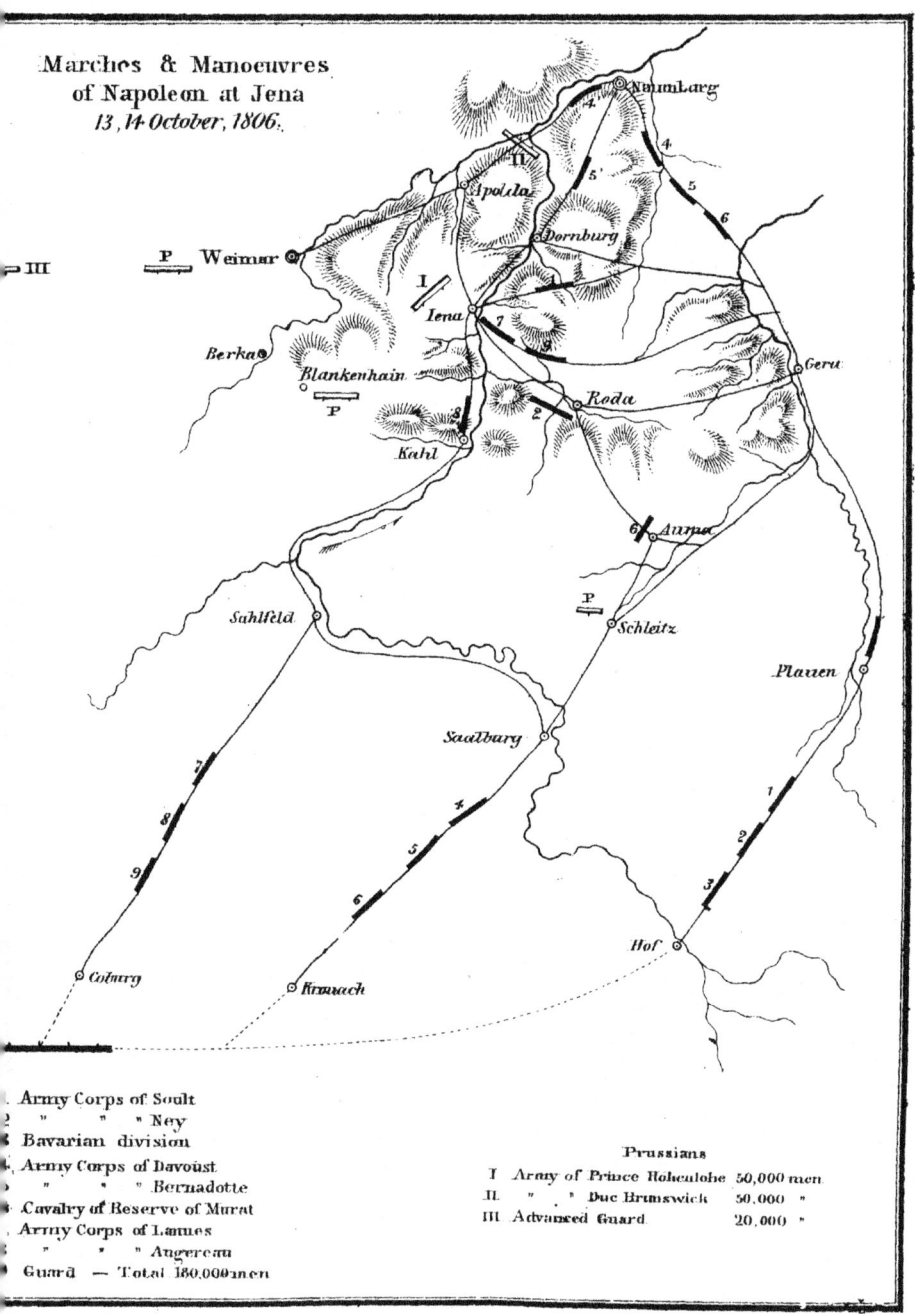

other corps; and, besides, the direction is always such that, wherever he attacks, he is outflanked. If he directs his efforts against Ney, who forms the pivot in the manœuvre, he is outflanked by Soult; and if he attacks the latter, Ney and Davoust are on his flanks.

The result of this manœuvre—which was, however, excellently favored by Mack's own incapacity—was the complete destruction of the Austrian army under his command.

I will say a few words on the repose of troops in time of war.

They bivouac, canton, or camp.

In the bivouac, they pass the night in the open air, round fires, etc.; in camping, they are provided with tents; in cantoning, they are distributed in houses among the inhabitants.

In the wars of Europe, the latter mode is always adopted for all kinds of marches and manœuvres.

Troops bivouac only when in expectation of a battle.

In all these cases, however, the arrangements must be so made that, from resting, the troops can quickly join and form in line of battle.

In camping, the tents should be disposed so that each battalion, brigade, division, etc. can form from its camp at once in line or in order for marching; advanced guards, posts, and pickets should be disposed, and the distances from the main body should be calculated the same as for columns in marching—that is, that the army should have time to assemble and form for battle. The disposition for camps will be found in all army regulations; and this, as well as the cantoning of troops, being the special mission of the officers of the general staff, it would be useless to say more here concerning it.

I trust that this summary will suffice to give the reader a general but a clear idea of the great operations of war. For special study, the works of General Jomini, Ternay, Frederick II., Archduke Charles, Loyd, Clausewitz, the Memoirs of Napoleon, Marshal Marmont, etc. etc. should be consulted.

THE END.

Marches & Manoeuvres of Napoleon near Ulm, 6 October 1805.

1	Army Corps of Ney		Soult
2	" " "		Murat
3	" " "		Lannes
4	" " "		Davoust
5	" " "		Marmont
6	" " "		Bernadotte

MILITARY BOOKS

PUBLISHED BY

J. B. LIPPINCOTT & CO.
PHILADELPHIA.

Major-General McClellan's Works.

The Armies of Europe: comprising descriptions in detail of the Military Systems of England, France, Russia, Prussia, Austria, and Sardinia. Adapting their advantages to all arms of the United States Service. Embodying the Report of Observations in Europe during the Crimean War, as Military Commissioner from the United States Government in 1855-56. By GEO. B. MCCLELLAN, Major-General U.S. Army. Originally published under the direction of the War Department, by order of Congress. 1 vol. 8vo. Illustrated with a fine steel Portrait and several hundred Engravings. $3.50.

This most interesting volume, prepared with great labor by General MCCLELLAN, from copious notes taken during his tour of observation in Europe, under orders from the War Department, opens to the reader much of his own military history and culture. Here will be found his matured views on subjects of immediate and absorbing interest, and the noble and bold suggestions contained herein he is now in position to realize, and is, in fact, every day applying in practice. The book is a striking prophecy, of which his present position and his assured fame are the bright fulfilment.

Regulations and Instructions for the Field Service of the U.S. Cavalry in Time of War. By GEO. B. MCCLELLAN, Major-General U.S. Army. To which is added, the Basis of Instruction for the U.S. Cavalry, from the authorized Tactics,—including the formation of regiments and squadrons, the duties and posts of officers, lessons in the training and use of the horse,—illustrated by numerous diagrams, with the signals and calls now in use; also, instructions for officers and non-commissioned officers on outpost and patrol duty. With a drill for the use of cavalry as skirmishers, mounted and dismounted. 1 vol. 12mo. Fully illustrated. $1.50

European Cavalry, including details of the organization of the Cavalry Service among the principal nations of Europe; comprising England, France, Russia, Prussia, Austria, and Sardinia. By GEO. B. MCCLELLAN, Major-General U.S. Army. 1 vol. 12mo. Fully illustrated. $1.25.

Manual of Bayonet Exercises. Prepared for the Use of the Army of the United States. By GEO. B. MCCLELLAN, Major-General U.S. Army. Printed by order of the War Department. 1 vol. 12mo. Fully illustrated. $1.25.

United States Infantry Tactics. For the Instruction, Exercise, and Manœuvres of the U.S. Infantry, including Infantry of the Line, Light Infantry, and Riflemen. Prepared under the direction of the War Department, and authorized and adopted by SIMON CAMERON, Secretary of War. Containing the School of the Soldier, the School of the Company, Instructions for Skirmishers, the General Calls, the Calls for Skirmishers, the School of the Battalion, the Articles of War, and a Dictionary of Military Terms. 1 vol. complete, illustrated with numerous Engravings. $1.25.

War Department, Washington, May 1, 1861.

This System of United States Infantry Tactics for Light Infantry and Riflemen, prepared under the direction of the War Department, having been approved by the President, is adopted for the instruction of the troops when acting as Light Infantry or Riflemen, and, under the act of May 12, 1820, for the observance of the militia when so employed.

SIMON CAMERON, *Secretary of War.*

Cooke's U.S. Cavalry Tactics. Cavalry Tactics; or, Regulations for the Instruction, Formations, and Movements of the Cavalry of the Army and Volunteers of the United States. Prepared under the direction of the War Department, and authorized and adopted by the Secretary of War, Nov. 1, 1861. By PHILIP ST. GEORGE COOKE, Brigadier-General U.S. Army. In two vols. 18mo. $1.50.

Vol. I. School of the Trooper, of the Platoon, and of the Squadron.
Vol. II. Evolutions of a Regiment and of the Line.

Revised Regulations for the Army of the United States. 1861. By authority of the President of the United States and the Secretary of War. With a full Index. 1 vol. 8vo. 559 pp. $1.75.

Jomini's Art of War.

The Art of War. By BARON DE JOMINI, General and Aid-de-Camp of the Emperor of Russia. A New Edition, with Appendices and Maps. Translated from the French by Capt. G. H. MENDELL, U.S.A., Corps of Topographical Engineers, and Lieut. W. P. CRAIGHILL, U.S.A., Corps of Engineers. Demi 8vo. $1.50.

A new translation is here presented of the well-known standard work of one of the ablest modern military critics and historians. It treats fully of strategy and tactics, of the relation of diplomacy to war, of various branches of military policy, and many other important topics connected with the science of arms. An excellent index and several supplementary essays enhance the value of the volume.—*N. Y. Tribune.*

In a small octavo volume, Jomini treats of strategy and tactics, grand tactics, the art of moving armies, and the formation of troops for battle, in a manner which the world has agreed to call *masterly*. . . . While everybody is criticizing the war, would it not be well for somebody to read this greatest of military critics, and know a mere smattering about the matters so dogmatically discussed? With the utmost diffidence or the utmost assurance, it might be convenient occasionally in conversation to back up an opinion by an allusion to the Baron de Jomini, General and Aid-de-Camp of the Emperor of Russia. *It must be confessed that he knows something about war.*—*Conn. Courant.*

It is a book to be *studied*, not skimmed. Jomini is the first of living military critics.—*The Press.*

To one who desires to be well informed on the principles, science, and art of war, this work is most invaluable.—*Chicago Journal.*

Marmont's Military Institutions.

The Spirit of Military Institutions; or, Essential Principles of the Art of War. By MARSHAL MARMONT, Duke of Ragusa. Translated from the latest edition, revised and corrected by the Author, with Illustrative Notes, by HENRY COPPÉE, Professor of English Literature in the University of Pennsylvania, late an Officer of Artillery in the Service of the United States.

This book contains, in a small compass, the principles of the art of war, as learned and practiced by this great marshal during the Napoleonic wars. It treats of strategy, tactics, and grand tactics,—of the organization and formation of armies,—the principles of fortification,—of military justice, wars offensive and defensive, marches and encampments, reconnoissances, battles,—and various important topics, including the tactics of the three arms as applied in actual movements before the enemy,—with the peculiar characteristics and duties of general officers.

4   J. B. LIPPINCOTT & CO.'S MILITARY PUBLICATIONS.

The Ordnance Manual, for the use of the Officers of the Army and others. Prepared under the direction of the War Department. Third edition. 1 vol. demi-8vo. Fully illustrated. $2.50.

CONTENTS.—CHAP. I. Ordnance. II. Shot and Shell. III. Artillery Carriages. IV. Machines, etc., for Siege and Garrison Service. V. Artillery Implements and Equipments. VI. Artillery Harness and Cavalry Equipments. VII. Paints, Lackers, etc. VIII. Small Arms, Swords, and Accoutrements. IX. Gunpowder, Lightning-Rods. X. Ammunition of all kinds, Fireworks. XI. Equipment of Batteries for Field, Siege, and Garrison Service. XII. Mechanical Manœuvres. XIII. Artillery Practice, Ranges, Penetration, etc. XIV. Materials, Strength of Materials. XV. Miscellaneous Information, Tables of Weights and Measures, Physical Data, Mathematical Formulæ, Ballistics, Tables, etc.

This most valuable work to persons engaged in the military service and in the preparation of any of the various military supplies, (the construction of which is given in minute detail,) will also prove useful to mechanics generally for the valuable tables and miscellaneous information which it contains.

Hardee's Rifle and Light Infantry Tactics, for the Exercise and Manœuvres of Troops when acting as Light Infantry or Riflemen. Prepared under the direction of the War Department. By Brevet Lieutenant-Colonel W. J. HARDEE, U.S.A. 2 vols. complete. VOL. I. Schools of the Soldier and Company; Instruction for Skirmishers. VOL. II. School of the Battalion. $1.50.

Henderson on the Examination of Recruits. Hints on the Medical Examination of Recruits for the Army, and on the discharge of Soldiers from service on Surgeon's Certificate. Adapted to the service of the United States. By THOMAS HENDERSON, M.D., Asst. Surgeon U.S. Army. A new edition, revised by RICHARD H. COOLIDGE, M.D., Asst. Surgeon U.S. Army. 1 vol. 12mo. $1.00.

A Manual of Military Surgery; or, Hints on the Emergencies of Field, Camp, and Hospital Practice. By S. D. GROSS, M.D., Professor of Surgery in the Jefferson Medical College of Philadelphia. 1 vol. 18mo. 50 cents.

Cavalry Tactics. Published by order of the War Department. FIRST PART.—School of the Trooper, of the Platoon and of the Squadron Dismounted. SECOND PART.—Of the Platoon and of the Squadron Mounted. THIRD PART.—Evolutions of a Regiment. 3 vols. 18mo. $3.75.

War Department, Washington, Feb. 10, 1841.

The system of Cavalry Tactics adapted to the organization of Dragoon regiments, having been approved by the President of the United States, is now published for the government of the said service.

Accordingly, instruction in the same will be given after the method pointed out therein; and all additions to, or departures from, the exercises and manœuvres laid down in this system are positively forbidden.
J. R. POINSETT, *Secretary of War.*

Instruction in Field Artillery. Prepared by a Board of Artillery Officers. 1 vol. demi-8vo. $2.50.

Baltimore, Md., Jan. 15, 1859.

COL. S. COOPER, Adjt. Gen. U.S.A.

SIR:—The Light Artillery Board assembled by Special Orders No. 134, of 1856, and Special Orders No. 116, of 1858, has the honor to submit a revised system of Light Artillery Tactics and Regulations recommended for that arm.
WM. H. FRENCH, Bt. Major, Captain First Artillery.
WILLIAM F. BARRY, Captain Second Artillery.
HENRY J. HUNT, Bt. Major, Captain Second Artillery.

War Department, March 6, 1860.

The system of instruction for Field Artillery, prepared by a Board of Light Artillery Officers, pursuant to orders from this Department, having been approved by the President, is herewith published for the information and government of the army.

All exercises, manœuvres, and forms of parade not embraced in this system are prohibited in the Light Artillery, and those herein prescribed will be strictly observed.

BY ORDER OF THE SECRETARY OF WAR.

The Handy-Book for the United States Soldier, ON COMING INTO SERVICE. Containing a Complete System of Instruction in the School of the Soldier; embracing the Manual for the Rifle and Musket, with a preliminary explanation of the Formation of a Battalion on Parade, the Position of the Officers, &c. &c. Also, Instructions for Street-Firing. Being a First Book or Introduction to the authorized United States Infantry Tactics. Complete in 1 vol. 128 pages, illustrated. 25 cents.

To the recruit just mustered into service, the system of tactics seems extensive and difficult.

The design of this little Handy-Book is to divide the instruction, and, by presenting a complete system for the drill of the individual soldier, to prepare him for the use and study of the authorized United States Infantry Tactics, in the school of the company and the battalion.

6 J. B. LIPPINCOTT & CO.'S MILITARY PUBLICATIONS.

Evolutions of the Line. Field Manual of Evolutions of the Line, arranged in a tabular form, for the use of officers of the United States Infantry; being a sequel to the authorized United States Infantry Tactics. Translated, with adaptation to the United States Service, from the latest French authorities, by Captain HENRY COPPÉE, late Instructor in the United States Military Academy at West Point. 18mo. 50 cents.

From Brigadier-General J. K. A. Mansfield, U.S.A.

I received in due time your little book of the "Evolutions of the Line." I am delighted with it. It is the best thing of the kind I have seen. It is concise, to the point in every particular, and deserves the exclusive patronage of the Government.

Manual of Battalion Drill. The Field Manual of Battalion Drill, containing all the movements and manœuvres in the School of the Battalion, with the commands arranged in tabular forms and properly explained. Translated from the French, with adaptation to the United States Service, by Captain HENRY COPPÉE, late Instructor in the United States Military Academy at West Point. 18mo. 50 cents.

From General George A. McCall, U.S.A.

Thank you for the two beautiful little volumes,—"The Field Manual of Battalion Drill," and the "Field Manual of Evolutions of the Line." I have examined them with great care, and I have much pleasure in assuring you that in my estimation you have brought forth the very best thing of its kind that could possibly have been produced at this particular time. Greatly condensed, it is still full enough to satisfy the student, and is, in fact, the best *vade-mecum* I have ever seen.

From General John E. Wool, U.S.A.

I am greatly obliged for the volumes of your "Field Manual of Battalion Drill" and "Evolutions of the Line." The arrangement is no less admirable than it is well calculated to aid the officer in acquiring with ease and facility the "battalion drill," as well as the "evolutions of the line." Altogether, I think them the best Field Manuals I have ever seen. I hope the whole army will be furnished with both volumes.

Manual for Courts-Martial. A Manual for Courts-Martial, containing full Explanations of the Duties of all Officers employed on such Service, with complete Forms of Proceedings. By Captain HENRY COPPÉE, late Instructor in the United States Military Academy at West Point. (Nearly ready.)

Guthrie's Surgery of War. Commentaries on the Surgery of the War in Portugal, Spain, France, and the Netherlands, from the battle of Roliça, in 1808, to that of Waterloo, in 1815, with additions relating to those in the Crimea, in 1854–55; showing the improvements made during and since that period in the great art and science of Surgery on all the subjects to which they relate. By G. J. GUTHRIE, F.R.S. One vol. 12mo. $2.25.

It is safe to say that no other living man has had so wide a range of experience in "military surgery" as the author of this work. There is scarcely another living name so familiar to the ears of surgeons as his. . . . We do not set out to praise or compliment this volume of Mr. Guthrie's, for we deem it unnecessary to "carry coals to Newcastle." We would only suggest that it is a book equally as valuable to the surgeon in civil life as to the military surgeon; and we know of no other surgical work which, in as limited space, conveys so vast an amount of inestimable information. It is not a catchpenny thrown upon the war-market, but one which will be ranked with the text-books and classics of professional literature.—*Chicago Medical Journal.*

Macleod's Surgery of the Crimean War. Notes on the Surgery of the War in the Crimea, with Remarks on the Treatment of Gunshot Wounds. By GEORGE H. B. MACLEOD, M.D., F.R.C.S., Surgeon to the General Hospital in Camp before Sebastopol, Lecturer on Military Surgery in Anderson's University, Glasgow, &c. &c. One vol. 12mo. $1.50.

I thank you for the copy of "Macleod's Surgery." With the English edition I am very familiar, and regard it as one of the best of the modern works on military surgery. Its republication at the present moment is a valuable contribution for our army surgeons, all of whom should have it. HENRY H. SMITH, *Surgeon-General of Pennsylvania.*

Altogether, this is a very interesting as well as useful work, and will be sought for eagerly by the profession.—*Lancet and Observer.*

Longmore's Gunshot Wounds. A Treatise on Gunshot Wounds. By T. LONGMORE, Deputy Instructor of Hospitals, Prof. of Military Surgery at Fort Pitt, Chatham. In two Parts:
Part I. Gunshot Wounds in General.
Part II. Gunshot Wounds in Special Regions of the Body.
One vol. 12mo.

Professor Longmore is one of the most eminent surgeons in the British army, and gained great experience in the Crimea on the subject of which this work treats. He had also the advantage of witnessing the practice of the best French surgeons in that dreadful campaign, and is fully qualified for the task he has undertaken,—that of laying down rules for the treatment of gunshot wounds. The reader will find material for study in every line.—*North American.*

8 J. B. LIPPINCOTT & CO.'S MILITARY PUBLICATIONS.

Willard's Target Practice. Manual of Target Practice for the United States Army. By Captain GEORGE L. WILLARD, U.S.A.

     WASHINGTON, D.C., *February* 19, 1862.

The undersigned recommend the system of Target Practice compiled by Captain George L. Willard, 8th Infantry, U.S.A., for the use of the Army.

It is essentially that already adopted by the War Department, and is adapted to the requirements of the troops now in the field. It is much needed.

 GEORGE SYKES,
  Major 14*th Infantry, U.S.A., and Brig.-Gen. U.S.V.*
 W. S. HANCOCK,
  Captain Staff, and Brigadier-General U.S.V.
 DANIEL BUTTERFIELD,
  Lieut.-Col. 12*th Infantry, U.S.A., and Brig.-Gen. U.S.V.*
 P. KEARNEY,
  (*Late Captain* 2*d Dragoons,*) *Brigadier-General U.S.V.*

Duffield's School of the Brigade and Evolutions of the Line. School of the Brigade and Evolutions of the Line; or, Rules for the Exercise and Manœuvres of Brigades and Divisions. Designed as a Sequel to the United States Infantry Tactics, adopted May 1, 1861. By WILLIAM W. DUFFIELD, Colonel Ninth Michigan Infantry. One vol. 18mo.

Schalk's Art of War. Summary of the Art of War, written expressly for, and dedicated to, the United States Volunteer Army. By EMIL SCHALK, A.O.

A LIBERAL DISCOUNT made to parties ordering by the quantity; or single copies will be forwarded by mail (post-paid) on receipt of the price, in gold or postage stamps, by the Publishers.

Constantly on hand, and for sale at wholesale or retail, a large stock of AMERICAN and FOREIGN MILITARY BOOKS, SCHOOL and COLLEGE TEXT-BOOKS, standard LAW, THEOLOGICAL, and MEDICAL works, and Miscellaneous Books of every department of Literature.

     J. B. LIPPINCOTT & CO.
       Philadelphia.

Printed in Dunstable, United Kingdom